FLORENCE NIGHTINGALE

FLORENCE NIGHTINGALE

The Courageous Life of the Legendary Nurse

CATHERINE REEF

CLARION BOOKS
HOUGHTON MIFFLIN HARCOURT | BOSTON NEW YORK

CLARION BOOKS
3 Park Avenue, New York, New York 10016

Copyright © 2017 by Catherine Reef

Clarion Books is an imprint of
Houghton Mifflin Harcourt Publishing Company.

www.hmhco.com

The text was set in Bell MT.
Book design by Sharismar Rodriguez

Library of Congress Cataloging-in-Publication Data
Names: Reef, Catherine, author.
Title: Florence Nightingale : the courageous life of
the legendary nurse / Catherine Reef.
Description: Boston : Clarion Books, [2017] | Audience: Ages 12+.
Includes bibliographical references and index.
Identifiers: LCCN 2015045606 | ISBN 9780544535800 (hardcover)
Subjects: LCSH: Nightingale, Florence, 1820–1910—Juvenile
literature. | Nurses—England—Biography—Juvenile literature.
Classification: LCC RT37.N5 R44 2017 | DDC 610.73/092—dc23
LC record available at http://lccn.loc.gov/2015045606

Manufactured in China
SCP 10 9 8 7 6 5 4 3 2 1
4500606678

For Sara Hoffee

CONTENTS

PROLOGUE	The Night Gallery	1
CHAPTER 1	"Mistress of All She Attempts"	7
CHAPTER 2	A Woman with Work to Do	20
CHAPTER 3	"Dust and Nothing"	35
CHAPTER 4	The Prison Called Family	48
CHAPTER 5	Shadows in a Thirsty Land	62
CHAPTER 6	"But One Person in England"	75
CHAPTER 7	The Horrors	90
CHAPTER 8	An Angel with a Lamp	105
CHAPTER 9	Nightingale Power	120
CHAPTER 10	Maid of All Work	136
CHAPTER 11	A Noble Life	150
NOTES		163
SELECTED BIBLIOGRAPHY		174
PICTURE CREDITS		177
INDEX		178

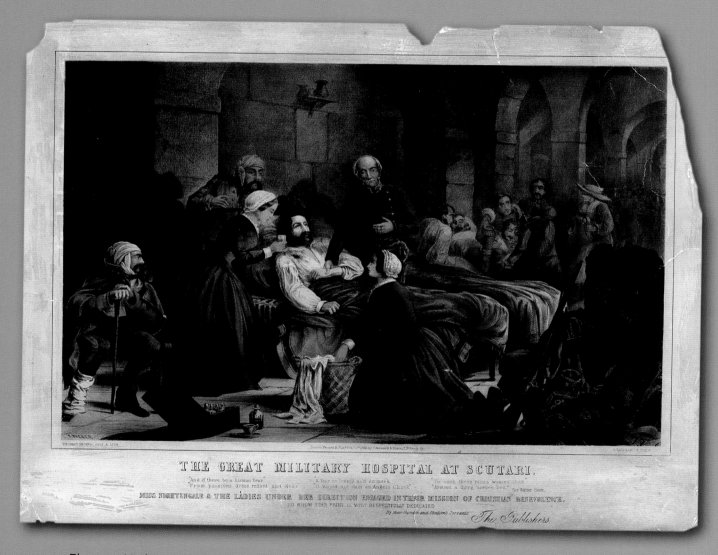

Florence Nightingale (standing) and another nurse comfort a dying soldier at the Barrack Hospital.

The Night Gallery

THINGS happening at night had the look of old paintings. Candles and hand-held lamps cast golden light on people quietly busy at their labor. Foreheads, cheeks, and hands glowed softly as if lit from within. Deep-hued garments fell away in shadow, while everything beyond the circle of light vanished into blackness.

Beautiful from a distance, the scenes were heartbreaking when viewed up close. In one, a British soldier whose arm had been blown off lay on a cracked stone floor. A chaplain and a medical officer hovered nearby as a woman dressed his wound. "War's work," said the chaplain, "is altogether an accursed work." On another night, the same nurse bound a stump, all that was left of a second soldier's leg, as a nun in a long veil sponged away blood.

The nurse giving aid on this dark night was Florence Nightingale. Thirty-four years old, tall and slender, she wore her reddish-brown hair tucked into a white cap. She had "a face not easily forgotten," noted the chaplain. It was "pleasing in its smile, with an eye betokening great self possession, and giving when she wishes, a quiet look of firm determination to every feature." Nightingale needed that determination — that grit. She had come to this place, the Barrack Hospital at Scutari, in northwest Turkey, as part of a great experiment. For the first time, the British army was employing female nurses in its wartime hospitals, and Nightingale was the nurse in charge.

It was 1854, and the two wounded soldiers were many miles from home. They held a different set of pictures in their minds: cavalry brigades riding toward one another across a bleak landscape, their bayonets raised; the chaos of battle—swords slashing, cannon firing, men tumbling to the ground; then, later, fallen horses and crushed wagons, bodies sprawled on hillsides with dead eyes staring at the sun.

Along with the Turkish and the French, the British were fighting the Crimean War. They were battling the Russians, who wanted greater influence on the Balkan Peninsula of southeast Europe. The brutal war was costing hundreds of thousands of lives. Men were killed in action, but many more died later from infection or disease. Some of the soldiers in Nightingale's care had waited days for a boat to carry them from camp or battlefield across the Black Sea to Scutari. After reaching the pier, they were loaded into carts or strapped onto mules to go the last quarter mile to the Barrack Hospital, crying out at every bump in the rough road.

Nightingale had arrived to find the hospital in a shameful state. Miles of sick and wounded men lined the corridors. In row after horrific row, they lay on the floor or on thin mattresses held up by rotting wood. Their foul blankets teemed with lice, and the stench of overflowing latrines poisoned the air. Meals were inedible and often served raw. "That this is the Kingdom of Hell no one can doubt," Nightingale declared. She and her nurses got busy, bringing order and cleanliness to the hospital and hope to the suffering men.

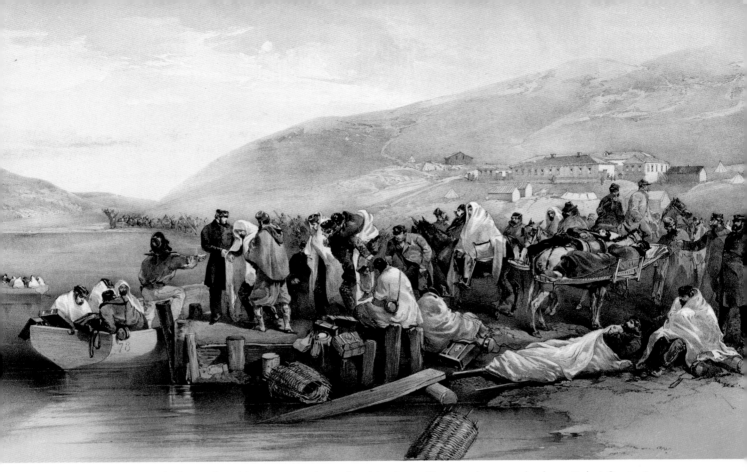

Sick and wounded British soldiers wait to board a ship that will carry them to the hospital at Scutari.

Florence Nightingale's work in Scutari earned her devotion from those at home and made her famous throughout the world. Her admirers wrote songs and poems about her. They bought Florence Nightingale statuettes to place on their mantels. They hung fanciful pictures of Nightingale visiting soldiers' beds, always carrying a lantern. People called her "the Lady with the Lamp."

Even today, Florence Nightingale is remembered for her service in the Crimean War. Yet wartime work took up less than two years of her life, and many of her significant accomplishments came later. She returned to England in 1856 with the coming of peace. Her health had been shattered by the war, but she kept working to bring people better medical care and further the training of nurses. Her efforts paved the way for the modern profession of nursing. With so much to do, she drove herself and others hard, and she had no patience for delays. "She always talks as if her time were short," said Dr. John Sutherland, a loyal colleague, yet she was to live a long time.

She was also a daughter and sister who was often at odds with those who loved her. She had pushed hard against her family's objections—and society's rigid rules—to create the life she felt called to live. Although a man could move freely in the world in the mid-nineteenth century, home was an English lady's realm. She was expected to be graceful, delicate, and virtuous and to make home a man's welcoming refuge. She obeyed her husband if she was married or her father if she remained single, regardless of her age.

Nightingale had dared to ask, "Why have women passion, intellect, moral activity—these

YOU ARE NEEDED NOW

JOIN THE
ARMY NURSE CORPS
APPLY AT YOUR RED CROSS RECRUITING STATION

A 1943 poster asks American women to enlist in the U.S. Army Nurse Corps during World War II. By the twentieth century, having female nurses serve in wartime hospitals—something controversial in Nightingale's day—had become standard.

Florence Nightingale defied her family's expectations to pursue a nursing career. This photograph was taken in 1853 or 1854.

three—and a place in society where no one of the three can be exercised?" Every time a person gave up a dream for social approval, "the world is put back," she believed.

Florence Nightingale wanted the world to move forward. She thought that in nursing, as in every human activity, "constant progress is the law of life."

CHAPTER 1

"Mistress of All She Attempts"

FANNY and William Nightingale married on a hot June day in 1818 and left for a long honeymoon in Italy. The following April, their first child was born in busy Naples, where craftsmen and housewives brought their work outdoors, into the streets. Fanny and William called their fragile daughter Parthenope (par-then-O-pee), for the ancient Greek settlement that once prospered on the spot where Naples stood. They waited through the cloudless summer and the rainy fall until Parthenope was strong enough to travel. By February she was thriving, so the family moved on to Florence, where gardens were soon to grow green and fragrant. Their second daughter was born there on May 12, 1820, and was named—what else? Florence.

The Nightingales went home to England when winter returned and moved into Lea Hurst, a great old house that William had inherited. Lea Hurst had belonged to William's great-uncle "Mad Peter Nightingale," a man remembered for his wild spirit. Mad Peter had loved to drink and gamble and race on horseback across the country-side at night, leaping over dark ditches and shadowy hedgerows. He never married and had no children, so when he died in 1803, his entire estate—Lea Hurst, the sur-rounding buildings and property, and a hundred thousand British pounds—passed

Shops crowd the Ponte Vecchio ("Old Bridge"), which spans the
Arno River in Florence, Italy, the city of Florence Nightingale's birth.

to his nephew, William Shore, who was then a boy of nine. For centuries in England, wealth had been measured in land. As a rule, the owner of an estate willed it to his oldest male heir as a way to keep the family's fortune intact. Mad Peter had decreed in his will that his heir must carry on the family name. So when William Shore turned twenty-one and took possession of the estate, he became William Nightingale.

Tall, slim William was nothing like Mad Peter. He was a mild man who looked forward to a quiet life of leisure. He hated discord and preferred to retreat to a private place—his library or his London club—rather than take sides in a conflict. William had studied at Cambridge University and liked nothing better than to think and read; he was devoted to "Books, Books, Books" and often wondered how he would ever pass the time without them.

William adored his wife, Fanny Smith Nightingale, who was known for her beauty. Fanny wore stylish clothes and had lush brown hair that fell in waves. She was full of life and loved parties and dancing. Fanny dreamed of being the mistress of a fine home, with rooms for many guests. She thought that Lea Hurst might better suit her needs if it could be remodeled. After all, it stood in a pretty spot, overlooking acres of parkland.

As workers added a wing and a chapel to this house, William designed new fireplaces for its rooms and a stone staircase to ascend from its front hall. A neighbor remarked, "The whole place, embosomed as it is amongst a profusion of beautiful trees . . . surrounded by its gardens and shrubberies, and the walls covered with a profusion of ivy and creeping plants, is one of the most charming and poetical spots we have ever visited." Florence Nightingale loved this house. As a small child she heard the gentle voice of the river Derwent as it flowed past her nursery window; the river would call to her in dreams when she was grown up and far from home.

Lea Hurst was in Derbyshire, in central England, where winters were cold and lonely. As Fanny watched Florence grow thin and listened to Parthenope's nagging cough, she decided that the girls missed the warmth of Italy. So in 1825 the Nightingales bought a second splendid home to the south, in fashionable Hampshire. This house, called Embley, was within sight of the sea. The water

Florence Nightingale loved Lea Hurst, her family's home in Derbyshire.

and salt air were sure to benefit the children's health. Having a home in Hampshire brought the Nightingales closer to London, where stylish people spent the social season, which began after Easter and ran through mid-August.

For as long as anyone could remember, English society had been divided into classes, with king and queen at the top and laborers and peasants at the bottom. The titled nobility—dukes, earls, and viscounts—perched just below the crowned heads. Next came the gentry, people who held some distinction, perhaps because they had been knighted or because they owned land that had been in their family for generations. Beneath the gentry but above the lowest classes were people whose money was earned through trade. This was where the Nightingales fit in. William Nightingale's family, the Shores, had long been bankers in the city of Sheffield. Fanny Nightingale's

To Fanny Nightingale, Embley, in Hampshire, was an ideal home for entertaining guests.

family, the Smiths, had traded in spices, tea, and sugar imported from British colonies around the world.

By the middle of the nineteenth century, the boundary that separated the landed gentry from those below them was breaking down. Middle-class families who had acquired wealth were living in gracious homes and using proper etiquette like people of a higher social rank. They were employing staffs of servants and hiring governesses to teach their children. In 1827 Mrs. Nightingale engaged Miss Sara Christie to instruct Florence and Parthenope—Flo and Parthe, or Pop, as she was sometimes known. Mrs. Nightingale praised Florence to the new governess, calling her "a shrewd little creature with a clear head which makes her thoroughly mistress of all she attempts." Parthe was different, though. "[She] has not shown any decided tastes excepting for flowers & poetry," Fanny Nightingale reported. Seven-year-old Flo had her own instructions for Miss Christie. "Parthe and I are so different, that we require different treatment," she said.

Throughout her life, Florence Nightingale would wonder how two sisters so close in age, raised in the same setting, could be so unlike each other. Flo was the child who wrote letters to her aunts and Grandmother Shore. She was the one who collected shells at the seaside and then looked up their scientific names in a book. Florence was forever "enquiring into the why & wherefore of everything," observed Parthe. At eight Parthe liked to draw and paint with watercolors. She filled sketchbooks with pretty scenes and portraits of her family. Her carefree, sometimes careless ways could get on Flo's nerves.

The girls took daily walks in all but the worst weather because their mother wanted them to have stamina. They performed exercises to strengthen their arms and wrists—they called this "doing arms." Fanny Nightingale was not the only

Mrs. Nightingale holds Florence on her lap in this portrait from the 1820s; Parthenope stands at her side.

mother in England who worried about weak arms. At Kensington Palace, the Duchess of Kent made sure that her little girl, Princess Victoria, lifted Indian clubs every day. And lest she grow up with wobbly ankles, Flo wore steel-lined boots until she was a teenager.

Both sisters played in the gardens and parkland surrounding each home. Florence picked flowers and pressed them into albums. She loved all the animals she encountered, from her pony, Peggy, to the busy nuthatches that perched upside down on tree trunks and the mice that made their nest in a mattress in an unused room. She would feel fond of animals all her life.

When they were at Embley, the Nightingales worshiped at the local Anglican church, St. Margaret's. The girls had been baptized in the Anglican faith, or Church of England, as babies. At Lea Hurst, though, they attended services with the Dissenters, people who had broken away from the Church of England because they disagreed with its doctrines. The Puritans who went to North America in the 1600s were an early Dissenting sect. There were others, including the Quakers and the Unitarians. William and Fanny Nightingale, although married in the Church of England, both came from Unitarian families. From an early age, Flo questioned what she was taught in church. When she was six, she devised a way to test her religion's truth. She

Florence rides her pony, Peggy. This watercolor was painted by Florence's cousin Hilary Bonham Carter, who was a talented artist.

wrote down each of her prayers and the date by which she expected God to answer it. In every case her prayer was ignored. God wanted the faithful to work for their rewards, she decided.

Mrs. Nightingale was one of ten sisters and brothers, so Flo and Parthe grew up amid aunts, uncles, and cousins. Aunt Joanna lived nearby in Hampshire with her husband, John Bonham Carter, and their many children. Flo had fun building a summer playhouse with her Bonham Carter cousins. She especially liked Hilary, who was almost her age. The Nicholsons—Aunt Anne, Uncle George, and another pack of cousins—lived in Hampshire as well. Their magnificent home, Waverley Abbey, made Lea Hurst seem modest.

All the Smith relatives gathered there every year to celebrate Christmas.

Uncle Octavius Smith, who had earned a fortune of his own by distilling whiskey, lived in London with his wife, Jane, and their flock of children. Their house sat next to the distillery, and the sweet odor of fermenting grain filled its rooms. When Florence came to visit, she giggled and whispered through a hole in her bedroom wall to her cousin Fred, who was on the other side. She and Fred felt a thrill when Uncle Oc led them up ladders to the top of his distillery, where they walked along a wide pipe.

Mrs. Nightingale had two unmarried sisters. Aunt Julia was full of energy. She was always rushing here and there to care for a sick loved one or work for a cause she supported, such as the abolition of slavery or education for women. Aunt Patty, the oldest, had been her father's secretary for many years, but her brilliant mind was capable of more. Lacking opportunity, she was often lonely and depressed. A grown-up Florence Nightingale described Patty as one of the countless women of the nineteenth century who had "gone mad for the want of something to do."

Mr. Nightingale had only one sibling, a sister named Mai (pronounced "My"), and she often visited the Nightingales at Lea Hurst. Mai's lack of fashion sense exasperated Fanny Nightingale. "She's got an oddness like nobody else," Mrs. Nightingale would mutter. But Mai and Flo understood each other. Mai called the little girl "as precious to me as any thing I possess," and Flo was devoted to her in return. When Flo learned, at age seven, that Mai was to marry Fanny's brother Sam Smith, she cried. How dare someone separate her from this beloved aunt! During the wedding at Sheffield Cathedral, she knelt between the bride and groom to keep them apart. Afterward there was a festive breakfast with cake and fruit at Grandmother Shore's house, and Flo felt confused. It was "at once the happiest and the *un*happiest day" she had ever spent in that house, she said. Three years later, when Aunt Mai gave birth to a son named Shore, Flo was enchanted. She doted on the little boy, calling him "our Baby" and "the son of my heart."

In such a big family, someone was always getting sick. The symptoms and the remedies given fascinated Flo. Beginning at age nine she kept a written record of family ailments, of Uncle Octavius's back pain and Parthe's tooth extraction. Occasionally

Flo herself was the patient. Parthenope remembered the time Flo had whooping cough. "Her thirteen dolls had it too—were found with pieces of flannel round their 13 necks," Parthe recalled. (Wrapping the neck to keep it warm was a common treatment for whooping cough.) As an adult, Florence Nightingale said, "The first idea I can recollect when I was a child was a desire to nurse the sick."

She called the weeks she spent in bed with whooping cough "the happiest time of my life." She was free of Miss Christie and the boring, repetitive work the governess forced her to do. Flo hated writing in her copybook more than anything else. Penmanship was her poorest subject, and practicing sentences like "Conscience is a faithful and prudent monitor" over and over left her weary and sad. If she balked, Miss Christie made her sit still until she had "the spirit of obedience," Flo reported, however long that took.

Around the time of Shore's birth, Miss Christie left the Nightingales' employ to marry. To Flo this was just as well. "She did not understand children," she later said of Miss Christie. Rather than hire another governess or send the girls away to school, Mr. Nightingale took charge of their education. From then on, he instructed his daughters in most subjects, and a hired teacher visited the house to give them lessons in music and drawing.

Only about a third of English children went to school when Florence Nightingale was growing up. No laws required children to attend school, and there was no public education system. Affluent families hired governesses or tutors or sent their sons and daughters to private boarding schools that charged tuition. These schools varied greatly in size and quality. A few were exclusive institutions for boys where students enjoyed every comfort and the faculty was well trained; others, for either boys or girls, were operated in private homes by teachers who might not have had much education themselves. Some charity schools taught poorer children, but these youngsters started working at an early age and spent just a few years in school, if they went at all.

Whether a boy of Flo's social rank was educated at school or at home, he studied challenging subjects that readied him for college. Schooling was different for a girl, who had to prepare herself for a life spent at home and in social gatherings. She practiced skills such as needlework, drawing, and music. She learned to speak French and read some poetry. Many people thought a girl lacked a boy's intelligence; too much study would make her unladylike.

Flo's father disagreed. He was sure that girls could handle the same lessons as boys. He schooled his daughters in Latin, classical Greek, history, geography, Italian, English grammar, and composition. Florence put in long hours with her books, sometimes waking well before sunrise to prepare her lessons. She welcomed the challenge and soon advanced beyond Parthenope. By sixteen Flo was often with her father in his study, tackling chemistry, physics, astronomy, and philosophy, while Parthe sat in the drawing room with her mother.

Mrs. Nightingale had fretted about Parthe's frailty ever since her birth. In early 1836 Parthe scared the whole family when she developed a high fever and a bad cough that refused to go away. Every day the local doctor used leeches to draw blood from her ailing body and put heated glass bulbs on her skin to raise blisters. Nothing helped, and Mrs. Nightingale worried about tuberculosis. But slowly, Parthe improved, and by summer she was well enough to be presented in London at St. James's Palace.

Her curtsy before King William IV would last only a few seconds, but Parthe practiced it for days. She had to bow her head and bend so deeply that one knee nearly touched the floor, and she had to do the whole thing gracefully, without wobbling.

Upon rising she had to back out of the room with the long train of her dress gathered over her arm, because one never turned one's back on the monarch. For her debut Parthe wore a dress of white, the traditional color, trimmed with tiny pink hyacinths.

Making this formal entrance into society was a momentous event in a girl's life. It signaled that she was eligible for marriage. During the coming social season, as she attended balls and dinner parties, she would dress to show off her best features. She would be on display to single men and their parents. All mothers and fathers hoped for their children to marry well, but the Nightingales felt an added urgency to see their daughters wed. If Mr. Nightingale were to die without a male heir, his entire estate—Lea Hurst, Embley, and everything else he owned—would pass to his sister, Mai Smith. Mad Peter had spelled out these terms in his will, and they were unchangeable. The Nightingales had no son, so they needed a grandson. Otherwise,

Couples dance at a ball held at the Royal Naval College, in the southern English city of Portsmouth, in 1865.

William Nightingale's wife and daughters could end up dependent on Mai's kindness for their support.

Fanny Nightingale attended to her children's futures and their health. She was in charge of two large houses, and she enjoyed a busy social life. Florence admired the easy way her mother managed it all. "Order & beauty sprang up under her steps," Florence said. Like other genteel ladies, Fanny Nightingale did charity work. Flo and Parthe saw her give parcels of food, clothing, and blankets to poor villagers living near Lea Hurst and Embley.

Flo followed her mother's example and visited the poor, often spending hours with the sick and dying. If Flo had not returned by evening, Mrs. Nightingale would take a lantern and go out to fetch her. Fanny Nightingale knew she would find her daughter sitting beside a sickbed in a humble cottage. More often than not, Flo would refuse to come home to dinner. What was a mother to think of such a peculiar girl?

Flo also nursed animals. After she became famous, many books and magazines repeated a story about young Florence Nightingale and a shepherd's collie named Cap. It went like this: When she was sixteen and walking near Embley, Flo came upon a frightful scene. Some boys had been throwing rocks at Cap and injured his leg. Believing the leg was broken and there was no hope for his dog, the shepherd planned to hang Cap; he knew no other way to end the animal's suffering. Flo hated the thought of the dog dying and was certain something could be done. She raced to a nearby church and summoned the Reverend Jervis Giffard. The clergyman examined Cap's leg and found that it was badly hurt, but no bones were broken. Flo wrapped the dog's leg in warm dressings, and in time Cap recovered. He lived out his life as an active sheepdog, although he ran on three legs. The story sounds like a legend, but the Reverend Giffard confirmed that it was true.

Roger could hardly believe his eyes.

Cap shows his bandaged leg to the surprised shepherd in this illustration from a 1909 children's book. Cap's proud nurse, young Florence Nightingale, kneels at his side.

If people were sick and needed Flo's help, her energy was boundless. When influenza struck Embley in January 1837, everyone fell ill except Flo, the cook, and Parthe, who happened to be staying with the Nicholsons. From morning until night, Flo hurried upstairs and down, tending to sick family members and servants. She popped in at the cottages of the surrounding village, which was "one mass of illness," as she informed Parthe in a letter. As the epidemic waned, Flo reported, "I have killed no patients, though I have cured few."

Then, on February 7, something happened to Flo while she was alone in her bedroom, something strange, wondrous, and mystical. It seemed to her that God spoke her name and called her to His service. At the time, she told no one; she feared her family might laugh off her experience as "the passing fancy of a heated imagination," she later wrote. But sixteen-year-old Flo was sure that the call had been real. Where God led, she would follow—for the rest of her life.

CHAPTER 2

A Woman with Work to Do

WHAT did God have in mind for her? Florence was still waiting for Him to reveal His plan when she sailed for Europe with her parents, Parthenope, and two servants. This trip marked the final phase of Flo and Parthe's education. In Europe they would be surrounded by art and historic architecture. They would meet cultured people and practice speaking French, Italian, and German. They would return to England with the polish and poise that only a year and a half on the European continent could give them.

Their boat, the *Monarch*, left Southampton, England, on the drizzly night of September 8, 1837. Too excited to sleep, Flo stayed up late and listened as a crew member told the chilling tale of the *Amphitrite*. In 1833 this ship was carrying one hundred and eight female convicts to a penal colony in Australia, where English prisoners often served their sentences. Twelve children, sons and daughters of the convicts, were also aboard. The ship sailed into a gale and ran aground off France, not far from where the *Monarch* was sailing. Two seamen and one convict made it to dry land, but everyone else on the *Amphitrite* was lost in the churning, unpitying sea.

Le naufrage de l'Amphitrite, by Ferdinand Perrot

Terrified women cling to anything on deck as the *Amphitrite* pitches and heaves in rough weather. The story of this 1833 shipwreck haunted Florence Nightingale on her journey to France.

Despite Flo's fear of a shipwreck, the *Monarch* docked safely at Le Havre, on France's northern coast, and the Nightingales continued their journey south. Flo and Parthe took turns riding on top of the carriage with their father when the weather was fine. Like other wealthy Britons, the Nightingales brought their conveyance with them and hired horses once they were in France. William Nightingale had designed the carriage and had it built in England. It was big enough to seat twelve people and needed six horses to pull it. As Parthe sketched the scenery, Flo filled a notebook with facts about the places they visited and the people they met. She jotted down the distances between cities, the family's arrival and departure times, and any other information she thought worth recording.

The Nightingales crossed France from north to south, covering about thirty-five miles a day. They passed through Chartres, famed for its medieval cathedral. They saw Avignon, a city surrounded by a stone wall from the 1200s, and Nîmes, the site of Roman ruins dating from the first century. The travelers followed routes lined with

olive trees and thickly planted mulberries. Beauty and history surrounded them, but the roads were rocky, the hotel food was badly cooked, and fleas greeted them in their beds. "We have some of us been rather cross & disagreeable," Parthe wrote to relatives in England, mentioning no names.

Everyone cheered up when the carriage reached Nice, on the Mediterranean coast, ten days before Christmas. Many English people stayed in Nice, which meant that the Nightingales found food and lodgings to their liking. They mingled with their fellow Britons at holiday parties.

In January the Nightingales moved on to Italy, and Flo was spellbound. Picturesque Genoa, forming a crescent around its harbor, was magnificent, she said. Quaint sounds—the brays of donkeys and the chimes of monastery bells—reached her ears. In Genoa, Pisa, Venice, and her birthplace, Florence, she danced at balls, including one given by a duke. She even fell in love—with music. In fact, she went "music-mad," she said. She took singing and piano lessons and heard operas several times a week with her mother. She announced that she could listen to Donizetti's opera *Lucrezia Borgia* every night for the rest of her life and never tire of it. It was "so beautiful, so affecting, so enchanting."

After nearly a year in Italy and a brief stay in Switzerland, the Nightingales made their way to Paris. They attended no parties in the French capital because all celebrations had been canceled; France was mourning the death of Princess Marie, a daughter of King Louis Philippe. The twenty-five-year-old princess had died of tuberculosis, a common killer in the nineteenth century. Rainy Paris, with its stone houses blackened by grime, seemed drab after beautiful Italy, Flo thought. She and her family joined the other tourists frequenting its cafés and exclusive shops on the Boulevard

The artist William White created this portrait of Florence (left) and Parthenope Nightingale in 1836, when the girls were teenagers.

Florence loved the beautiful harbor at Genoa, graced by what was then the tallest lighthouse in the world.

des Italiens. They also enjoyed meeting Elizabeth Hay Clarke, an Englishwoman of advanced age who knew Flo's aunt Patty.

Mrs. Clarke's daughter, Mary, acted as the Nightingales' guide on outings to galleries, concerts, and the theater. Mary Clarke overflowed with talk. Her knowledge of art and books made her popular with Paris intellectuals, who often gathered in her drawing room for evenings of conversation. Mary Clarke was forty-five and unmarried; she was small and sprightly and carelessly dressed. Her hair fell into her face, causing one friend to joke that Mary and his terrier had the same hairdresser. Mary Clarke delighted in Parthe and Flo, who were "like May breezes" to her, she said. She asked them to call her Clarkey. Watching Clarkey, Flo saw a woman unafraid of breaking society's rules, one who pushed her way through crowds and mingled with men as their equal.

Mrs. Nightingale was watching her daughters. She wondered why they were "not more worshipped" by everyone they met. After all, Parthe spoke French very well; "even the French tell her occasionally that she has no accent," Fanny Nightingale wrote to her sister Julia. "Florence is much more admired for her beauty and she, too, is reckoned very clever and amusing." Yet, Mrs. Nightingale admitted, Florence's "stately manners keep people at a distance." Fanny's letter about Florence closed with a worried mother's prediction: "I do not expect that love passages will be frequent in her life."

The Nightingale sisters' unconventional friend Mary Clarke sketched this picture of herself.

People knew immediately that Flo and Parthe were sisters because, even though they had different interests, they looked very much alike. They were both slim and tall—Flo stood five feet, eight inches. They had similar features and both had auburn hair. But while friends complimented Flo's perfect teeth and graceful movements, they were silent about Parthe. Sickliness had dulled Parthe's looks. She was judged to be plain, which was an unfortunate thing for a girl to be when her future depended on making a good match. The friends also agreed among themselves that neither sister possessed her mother's great beauty.

The Nightingales returned to England in April 1839 and spent several weeks in London at the Carlton Hotel. Mrs. Nightingale was busy "from morning till night," she told her mother-in-law, "hiring servants & chusing papers & carpets & curtains for our new rooms." She and her husband had arranged for Embley to be enlarged and brightened up while they were in Europe, and the work was still going on. When it was finished, the Nightingales would be able to welcome five couples at a time as houseguests and still have room for their servants and luggage. William Nightingale, wanting a way to escape from all this company, insisted that his study have a secret entrance hidden by bookshelves.

In early May, Fanny Nightingale tore herself away from home decorating because Florence was to make her debut. She was to be presented at court, but she would not curtsy before King William IV. On June 20, 1837, William had died of heart failure. Succeeding him on the throne was his niece Princess Victoria, then a mere girl of eighteen. She was the same age as Parthenope.

Queen Victoria was to reign for sixty-four years, a period that came to be called the Victorian age. During these years, Britain's colonial empire grew, and so did its wealth and influence. Victorian England gave the world great writers such as Charles Dickens and the Brontë sisters. British inventors came up with the telephone, light-sensitive photographic paper, the pedal bicycle, and the flushing toilet. Thriving middle-class families filled their homes with knickknacks and curios. They placed lacy cloths called antimacassars on the backs and arms of chairs to keep the upholstery clean. Their solid furniture stood for stability, but they lived in a time of great change.

The factories that churned out pretty items for people to buy blackened industrial cities like Manchester. Slums grew around these cities as the promise of jobs drew workers from the countryside. Advances in scientific thinking, especially Charles Darwin's theory of evolution by natural selection, caused people to question their belief in God and their role in the universe.

This momentous era was just beginning when Florence Nightingale entered the queen's drawing room wearing a white dress purchased in Paris. She felt less frightened than she'd thought she would. "The Queen looked flushed and tired, but the whole sight was very pretty," she informed her loved ones.

Victoria was only eighteen years old when she became queen of England.

Flo's vivacious cousin Marianne Nicholson was also presented at court that year. She too was staying at the Carlton, along with her parents and sister Laura. Like Flo, Marianne cared more about making music than just about anything. According to Flo, "one unlucky piano never stopped" as she, Marianne, and Laura had lessons with music masters and took turns practicing. All day long, they played, sang, and danced, filling the Carlton's corridors with sound. Parthenope, who lacked musical talent, complained of illness.

In September, when the rest of the family moved back into Embley, Parthe went with the Bonham Carters to Harrogate, a spa in northern England. Harrogate was

Making music was a common pastime in the nineteenth century. By knowing how to play a musical instrument, a young woman could entertain herself and her family and friends. Musical skill might also add to her charms and help her attract a husband.

Parthe painted this watercolor sketch of Florence (left) and their cousin Marianne Nicholson at Embley.

a vacation spot, but drinking the iron-rich water that sprang from the ground there was believed to strengthen the sickly. (The Victorians placed great faith in water as a cure for their ailments.) Flo's letters helped Parthe imagine their newly remodeled home.

Heavy rain flooded roads and made traveling slow on moving-in day. The Nightingales' carriage went "to and fro upon the earth, or rather upon the water all day," Flo wrote. After arriving and changing into dry clothes, she and her parents looked around. "The house does not strike us as very large though there are so many new rooms," Flo reported to Parthe. She found much to praise, however, noting that the drawing room was "the admiration of all beholders." "The garden room is one of the prettiest in the house," she wrote. And the room where Aunt Mai was to sleep, "the yellow room, is as *light* as the outdoors."

Some renovations were less successful. Mrs. Nightingale hated the green wallpaper she had chosen for the music room and several bedrooms. (Flo disagreed. "The green is cheerful," she said.) Also, Flo warned Parthe that the bookcases were a failure because "the cupboards under them are shabby." Their parents were painfully aware of this shoddiness, so Flo advised her sister, "Silence is the best comment."

Florence was often in the music room, but she discovered another passion when her cousin Henry Nicholson paid a visit. Henry, a student at Cambridge, showed her the joys of algebra. The two spent hours together figuring out the values of x and y in complex equations. Flo envied Henry, who would continue his studies when he returned to college. As a girl, she could not go herself; she could only imagine what college was like. Her mind was as quick as Henry's, and she was just as capable of learning. So she asked her mother if she could study mathematics with a tutor.

Mrs. Nightingale dismissed the idea without giving it a second thought. A woman had no use for mathematics, she said. Flo appealed to her father, but he was no help at all. He was determined to stay out of disagreements that erupted between his wife and daughters.

Needing support from someone who understood her, Flo turned to Aunt Mai. Often, when they were together, Flo and Mai woke up early to study history and German. Mai had watched Flo explain algebra to her little cousin Beatrice. She knew that Flo thirsted for knowledge and cautioned Fanny Nightingale against forcing Flo to be bored. "If Flo were my own daughter, I should be very restless to see her immediately hard at work," she said. Mai had discussed Flo's situation with her husband, Sam Smith, and they both agreed that if Flo channeled her time and energy into mathematics instead of needlecraft and music, she might someday make strides in one of the sciences. Sam mentioned optics, the study of light and lenses.

For a woman to pursue science in the mid-nineteenth century was rare, but it was not unheard-of. Scottish-born Mary Somerville had written textbooks on physics and astronomy. Somerville had the public's approval because despite her scientific accomplishments, she had time to be a devoted wife and mother. The poet William Sotheby praised her as "thou, in whom we love alike to trace / the force of reason, and each female grace."

Fanny Nightingale was on the verge of changing her mind, but an obstacle remained. Where would Florence have these lessons? Bringing a master into their home to tutor Flo would cause too much disruption, she said. In truth, the disruption Flo's mother feared was of the romantic kind. If Flo worked closely with a tutor—who was likely to be a smart man without money—the two might fall in love. This could only be disastrous, because Florence needed to marry well, for the family's sake as well as her own.

Mary Somerville distinguished herself as an author of scientific books at a time when learned women were held in low esteem.

At Christmastime, news reached England that made Flo's problem seem small. Her cousin Fred Smith, Uncle Octavius's son, had died while on an expedition in northwestern Australia. After heavy surf damaged the team's boats and washed away most of its supplies, the eleven men began the long walk to the city of Perth, three hundred miles away. Hungry and thirsty, they trekked through thick woods and across barren plains that were red with ironstone. They felt lucky when they shot a hawk or a cockatoo for food or found fresh water. All the men survived the journey—all except one. After days with nothing to eat or drink, Fred crawled into the brush and died. He was nineteen, the same age as Flo.

Fred's grieving mother, Flo's aunt Jane, was soon to give birth to her seventh child and needed comfort and help. Aunt Julia, who often nursed family members, was caring for her ailing mother and unable to go. So Uncle Oc turned to Flo. He and Jane were fond of Flo; she and Fred had been playmates. Would Florence come to London and help her aunt?

For Flo the request came at just the right time. She needed to get away, and she needed something to do. In the house that smelled of fermenting grain, Flo played with her young cousins while Aunt Jane rested. She brought cushions and did what she could to make her aunt comfortable. She sat and listened when the heartbroken

An unknown artist captured this image of Florence Nightingale around 1840.

woman wanted to talk. For the first time in her life, she said, she felt she was "doing some little good."

She also studied mathematics. Fanny had relented and had given Flo permission to work with the Reverend Gillespie, a Presbyterian minister who had been Fred's tutor. There was no chance that Florence would be carried away by love. She found Gillespie unattractive—"a most awful man," she told her mother and sister—although she liked hearing him speak about Fred. She did her homework at night, after Aunt Jane and the children were asleep.

Parthe informed Clarkey that Florence had taken up mathematics. "And, like everything she undertakes, she is deep in them and working very hard," Parthe wrote. Soon Flo was schooling her cousin William Nicholson, who was preparing to enter the Royal Military Academy. Her uncle George Nicholson swore her to secrecy, because William would be ridiculed if his peers found out he had received lessons from a woman. After Aunt Jane safely gave birth to a girl named Edith, Flo's task in London was done, and she went to Lea Hurst for the summer.

As the pretty, accomplished daughter of a man with means, Flo was bound to have suitors, despite her mother's worries. One was named Marmaduke Wyvill. He played chess avidly, and his family had known the Smiths for many years. He had seen the Nightingales during their trip abroad, when they stayed at Nice in 1837. While visiting Lea Hurst in August 1840, he told William Nightingale of "the very great love & affection that has been inspired in me for your second daughter." He was bold enough to send Florence a marriage proposal: "If I am not mistaken by your manner & looks, then happiest am I of all mortals, but trembling do I wait to hear that you will confide yourself to my care & allow me to become your protector and guardian." Mr. Wyvill was woefully mistaken.

Another suitor stood a better chance. Richard Monckton Milnes was a poet and member of Parliament. He was a small, pleasant man with dark blond hair and a ruddy face. He had traveled throughout Europe, and he was intelligent and well connected in society. Mrs. Nightingale, eyeing him as a future son-in-law, invited him for the first of several stays at Embley. After he left, she wrote, "We all liked him and thought him unpretending."

Florence liked Milnes's commitment to social causes. It pleased her that he had spoken out against capital punishment. She listened when he read aloud from his

Richard Monckton Milnes is shown here in later life. In 1863 Milnes was made a baron and was thereafter known as Lord Houghton.

poetry, and she laughed at his clever jokes. She felt warmly toward him, but whenever Milnes spoke of marriage, she avoided giving him an answer. She was starting to think that a woman like herself, with "a work of God to do in the world," ought to remain single. There was no equality in marriage when it came to vocations, she had observed. As she explained to Hilary Bonham Carter, "Ladies' work has always to be fitted in"—fitted in after the needs of a husband and children have been met and the duties of keeping a household have been fulfilled. Yet "where a man is, his business is the law."

Florence's belief that God had called her to serve was as strong as ever. He seemed to have given her opportunities to serve the sick, and she had found satisfaction in the work. She now believed that God was leading her toward nursing.

CHAPTER 3

"Dust and Nothing"

IN the fall of 1844, an American couple traveling in England, Dr. Samuel Gridley Howe and his wife, Julia, spent a few days with the Nightingale family at Embley. Samuel Gridley Howe directed the Perkins Institution, a school for the blind in Boston. "We found a fine mansion," recalled Julia Ward Howe, "and a cordial reception. The family consisted of father and mother and two daughters, both born during their parents' residence in Italy." Of the daughters, "Parthenope was the elder; she was not handsome, but was piquant and entertaining. Florence was rather elegant than beautiful; she was tall and graceful of figure, her countenance mobile and expressive, her conversation most interesting."

Florence saw an opportunity in this visit. She wanted an honest opinion of her ambition from someone outside the family who had no wish to see her married. She took a chance and spoke to Dr. Howe. During a private conversation with Flo in the library, Howe acknowledged that her wish to practice nursing was unusual. But he said, "Go forward, if you have a vocation for that way of life; act up to your aspiration, and you will find that there is never anything unbecoming or unladylike in doing your duty for the good of others."

The Howes admired Florence enough to name their second daughter after her, but to Samuel Gridley Howe, Florence Nightingale remained an exception to the rule. Although he believed that she should pursue a career, he was less willing to see other women, including his wife, achieve outside the home. Julia Ward Howe recalled his saying that "if he had been engaged to Florence Nightingale, and had loved her ever so dearly, he would have given her up as soon as she commenced her career as a public woman."

Julia Ward Howe defied her husband to become a public woman. She joined the abolitionist movement and published her poetry. She is best remembered for composing the lyrics to the "Battle Hymn of the Republic." She and Samuel Gridley Howe separated in 1852.

Made bold by Dr. Howe's encouragement, Flo put together a plan. She would spend three months at the Salisbury Infirmary, a hospital thirteen miles from Embley, learning from its chief physician, Dr. Richard Fowler, who was the Nightingales' friend. Then she would find a small house to be the headquarters of a sisterhood of women like herself, educated ladies devoted to nursing. For more than a year, Flo told no one of her intentions. She revealed them to her family in December 1845.

After hearing what she had in mind, her parents and sister looked at one another in disbelief. The whole notion was unthinkable! The idea of Florence, an Englishwoman from a good family, venturing into hospital wards was simply absurd. Angry shouting broke out. Treating a dog with an injured leg or caring for an ailing aunt was one thing. Mingling with the lower classes was another matter altogether, argued Mrs. Nightingale and Parthe. Why, in an infirmary Flo might hear indecent words spoken or be confronted with vulgar behavior. The hard work required might destroy her own health.

Florence was displaying vanity, declared Mr. Nightingale, who for once took a side in a family quarrel. She was also being selfish. A woman's ambition was worth nothing when weighed against the happiness of those she loved. Having spoken his mind, Flo's father left for the quiet of his London club.

Twenty-five-year-old Flo felt the burn of bitter tears. Was it vanity to want more from life than tea and needlework? Was it selfish to dedicate oneself to serving the sick? Florence had a mission. She felt it; she knew it. She had opened her soul and revealed her dream only to have her family reject it out of hand.

Flo retreated to her room, to the privacy of pen and paper. "Forgive me, O God, and let me die, this day let me die," she wrote. Looking ahead to idle years was too much to bear. "I shall never do anything, and am worse than dust and nothing," she confided to the page. "Oh for some strong thing to sweep this loathsome life into the past."

Her parents may have seemed callous, but they had valid reasons for saying no to her plan. Hospitals were dirty, disgusting places. The Salisbury Infirmary, where Flo wanted to study, housed a thriving colony of rats. Rich people stayed away from hospitals, preferring to be treated at home when they were ill. Even the poor went to hospitals only if they had no one to care for them and nowhere else to go.

The nurses who worked in hospitals had no training. They were more like servants than health-care professionals. They cleaned the wards, washed the patients' clothes, emptied chamber pots, and carried away dirty bandages. Hospital nurses were often widows and single mothers who needed a means of support. Some were older women who had failed as household servants. Many nurses drank, and some engaged in sex work. There were a few nursing sisterhoods with good reputations, however. Flo had heard of the Deaconess Institute in Kaiserswerth, Germany, which trained Protestant women to nurse the sick and poor. For these sisters, nursing was religious work.

Florence calmed down, but she refused to be defeated. In mid-January she tried again. She wrote a letter to her father, who had been her zealous teacher just a few years before. He was not to laugh at her "poor little hope," she cautioned, because it deserved to be taken seriously. She was willing to compromise, though. If studying at the Salisbury Infirmary was out of the question, then perhaps she could spend a few months at a hospital in Dublin, where the nurses were Roman Catholic nuns. In that way, "there would not be the same

Charles Dickens based the character Sairey Gamp in his 1843 novel *Martin Chuzzlewit* on an actual nurse who had been described to him. Mrs. Gamp drinks heavily, and when drunk she carries on conversations with an imaginary friend.

objections as in an English Hospital." She wrote, "If you do believe it impossible to approve, I had rather know at once, & then, let us never speak on this subject again." How Mr. Nightingale responded to this letter is unknown, but he appears to have withheld his consent.

So Flo tried a different strategy. The best way to deal with her parents, she decided, was to be like the moon orbiting the earth. The moon stays close to the planet, "never leaves her," Flo knew. So from breakfast through dinner, she acted like the moon. She was a dutiful daughter, revolving around family and home.

Yet the earth sees but one face of the moon, Flo understood. "The other side remains forever unknown." From this moment on, Flo had a second side as well, one she revealed only when she was alone. She began rising early in the morning, while the rest of the household slept, to study reports on hospitals and health care. These were surprisingly easy to obtain, because government bodies such as the Poor Law Commission printed thousands of copies of their findings.

In her room Florence read of high death rates from disease—typhus, smallpox, consumption, pneumonia, and other illnesses. Many experts thought these diseases arose from unclean living conditions. Florence read of people dwelling near open sewers or in cottages with decaying thatched roofs that let in rain and snow. She learned of families sleeping in crowded rooms without ventilation and of open drains flowing past people's front doors, carrying all kinds of smelly waste and trash. "Filth and poverty go hand-in-hand without any restriction and under no control," one report noted.

Florence did her best to keep up the appearance of a cultured young English-woman in the eyes of others. She read the latest books, including *Jane Eyre*, a novel that was causing much comment. It was written by Charlotte Brontë, then an unknown

The actress Charlotte Thompson portrays Jane Eyre in a nineteenth-century play based on Charlotte Brontë's novel. Florence Nightingale had met women like Jane—strong and passionate yet unlikely to attract notice.

author from a remote part of England who hid behind a masculine pen name, Currer Bell. *Jane Eyre* tells the story of a small, plain governess who triumphs over abuse and obscurity and finds love. To Nightingale, Brontë's honest portrayal of a passionate woman made Jane Eyre seem real. "We know her—we have lived with her, we shall meet her again," she wrote to Julia Ward Howe.

With Richard Monckton Milnes, Flo went to London museums and scientific lectures sponsored by the British Association for the Advancement of Science. She tutored her younger cousins Shore Smith and William Bonham Carter. She also continued her good works, aiding the sick and poor near Lea Hurst and Embley and teaching in local charity schools. Still, she felt bored, unfulfilled, and sad. She sat with her family night after night, stitching and listening as someone read aloud. She wearily watched the clock, waiting for the magic moment, ten p.m., when she could slip away to her room.

By October 1847, she was finding it impossible to go on living this way. She tossed at night instead of sleeping, and lay in bed during the day. Her worried family watched her grow thin and nervous. Aunt Mai sought advice from a physician, who diagnosed "slow circulation" caused by "depression of spirits." Mai told Flo's mother that this doctor advised a change, one "calculated to make her life interesting & cheerful."

Help came from some friends of the Nightingales', Charles and Selina Bracebridge. They were going to Rome for the winter, and they invited Florence to come along. Flo's parents and her sister let out big sighs of relief. They hoped this trip would restore Flo's health and make her forget this foolish plan of becoming a nurse. "Yes, dear," Parthenope wrote to a cousin, "God is very good to provide such a pleasant time, and it will rest her mind, I think, entirely from wearing thoughts." Mr. Nightingale took out his big map of Rome and pointed out places he remembered from his honeymoon that Flo must be sure to see.

Flo knew what her loved ones were thinking, but she agreed that a winter in Italy would make her strong again. Also, she liked the Bracebridges, a childless couple in their forties. Charles Bracebridge immersed himself in the lore of England's past. He claimed to be a descendant of Lady Godiva, the eleventh-century noblewoman who, it was said, rode naked on horseback through the town of Coventry, covered only by her long hair. Lady Godiva's husband had dared her to make this ride, promising in exchange to lower the townspeople's taxes—or so the story went.

Selina Bracebridge was fascinated with the ancient world, especially early Greece. More important for Flo, she understood the workings of the human soul. She perceived that troubles had caused her young friend's ill health. She coaxed from Flo the story of her desire to pursue nursing and her family's objections. Then she offered her support to the girl. When a person is in despair, "God Himself is at a distance," a grateful Florence Nightingale later remarked. "But given one heart of fellow-feeling and the scene changes." Flo soon counted the Bracebridges among her closest friends. Selina was "more than a mother to me," she said.

Florence felt too weak to do much for herself, so Parthenope packed her trunks. Watching, Flo observed that she and her sister were still so different. Parthe seemed suited to the role society expected of her. She appeared to be "in unison with her age, her position, her country," Flo noted. "She is a child playing in God's garden & delighting in the happiness of all His works, knowing nothing of human life but the English drawing room, nothing of struggle in her own unselfish nature."

Parthe stayed at home in late October as Flo and the Bracebridges crossed the English Channel. Flo brought along a French maid, Mariette, who would help her dress and arrange her hair each morning. The travelers came ashore at Le Havre and went straight to Paris, where Flo had a long chat with her friend Clarkey. Mary Clarke was now Madame Mohl, having married Julius Mohl, a German scholar. From Paris, Flo, the Bracebridges, and Mariette traveled by carriage, boat, and train to the southern port of Marseille, where they boarded the ship that transported them to Italy. The final leg of the journey was the most beautiful, as the travelers rode in a carriage across the Italian countryside at night, under a ceiling of stars.

The Bracebridges belonged to the Nightingales' social circle, but their tastes differed from those of Flo's parents, and this suited their young companion just fine. Whereas Fanny insisted on stylish, resplendent lodgings when traveling, the Bracebridges sought an out-of-the-way place that was authentically Italian. They took rooms with large windows that let in the sun, rooms that could be reached only by climbing a treacherous staircase. One day, Charles Bracebridge fell down those stairs and hit his head. He bled quite a bit, but the injury was minor.

The Bracebridges avoided parties and devoted themselves to seeing sights and savoring Italian life. With Flo they stood in awe inside St. Peter's Basilica, the massive Renaissance cathedral where thousands often gathered to be led in prayer by the pope. Together the three toured the scenes of Rome's past glory, including the Forum, where centuries before, soldiers marched and emperors spoke to crowds. Of the temples that once surrounded this plaza, only moss-topped columns remained. Florence and the Bracebridges wandered through the quiet passageways of the Colosseum, the great arena where eighty thousand spectators once cheered as gladiators battled. Some days, Flo and Selina purchased hot roasted chestnuts from street vendors to snack on while they walked.

They went often to the Sistine Chapel. In the 1500s, the Italian master Michelangelo had covered the chapel's high ceiling with glorious frescoes—murals painted on wet plaster. In brilliant colors he had brought to life stories from the Bible with figures that celebrated the beauty of the human body. "Looking up into that heaven of angels and prophets," Flo wrote to her family in England, "I did not think that I was looking at pictures, but straight into Heaven itself." In the warmth of Italy's sun and the company of friends who accepted

Florence and the Bracebridges explored the ruins of the Colosseum in Rome.

Sidney Herbert, a leading English statesman of the nineteenth century, was to become Florence Nightingale's close friend.

Elizabeth Herbert shared Florence's interest in hospitals.

her, Florence felt her strength and happiness return. Soon Selina Bracebridge was writing to Mrs. Nightingale, "I think you would be *content* if you could see dear Flo's improved looks."

The Bracebridges introduced Florence to Sidney and Elizabeth Herbert, a couple on their honeymoon. Sidney Herbert was a nobleman's son and a member of Parliament. At thirty-seven, he was on his way up in the world, having served as secretary to the admiralty and secretary of war. He and Elizabeth, or Liz, were a handsome, charming couple who took an immediate liking to Flo. Intrigued by Flo's broad knowledge—so unusual in a woman of that time—Sidney Herbert engaged her in conversation.

With Liz Herbert at her side, Florence toured Italian hospitals. What the women saw discouraged them. At the San Giacomo Hospital, many patients were crowded into a single ward in four long rows of beds, "the stench dreadful, the locale cold, airless, dark," Florence wrote to Parthe. Patients stretched out their hands to beg as the two Englishwomen passed by. Conditions were a little better at the San Gallicano Hospital, which housed children with tuberculosis. At least there were bathtubs and a laundry. "But still no gardens, no place for air or exercise or anything to cure the children," Flo noted. The best thing to do with these hospitals, she concluded, would be to tear them down.

Through the Herberts, Flo met Mary Stanley, the daughter of an Anglican bishop. Seven years older than Nightingale, Stanley was also searching for a mission in life. She was on a spiritual journey as well and was in Rome because she felt drawn to the Roman Catholic faith. Florence and Mary Stanley would one day meet again.

Her natural curiosity drove Florence to study Catholic teaching and attend Mass, but she had no wish to join the church. On February 6, 1848, she was at an evening prayer gathering at St. Peter's. As the faithful asked for God's blessing, Florence noticed a small girl in the crowd. She was one of the many poor children who asked for handouts on the streets of Rome. Flo returned to her lodging, but she kept thinking of this helpless child. In the following days, she tracked down the girl, five-year-old Felicetta Sensi. Felicetta was living with someone who claimed to be her aunt, but Florence mistrusted this woman, who gave no thought to Felicetta's well-being. Determined to protect the child, Florence took the unusual step of enrolling her in a convent school herself. She would pay Felicetta's tuition during the coming years with money saved from her clothing allowance.

Florence found a friend in Madre Santa Colomba, the round, cheerful, open-hearted nun in charge of the convent school. Madre invited Florence to observe the school, and soon she let the young Englishwoman enter the convent for a spiritual retreat. For ten days, Florence withdrew from the wider world to contemplate her beliefs and goals. Madre counseled Florence to be strong when facing her family's resistance. "What does it matter even if we are with people who make us desperate?" she asked. "So long as we are doing God's will, it doesn't matter at all." About Florence's claim that she had been chosen by God, Madre said, "He calls you to a very high degree of perfection. Take care. If you resist, you will be very guilty." Florence was never to see the wise nun again, but she remembered her words during the trying months that followed.

Spring came, and Florence and the Bracebridges returned to England. Flo reached Embley refreshed by the Italian winter, but before long, she felt low again. The atmosphere at home was as exciting as "a warm bath," she complained. She fought off depression by visiting her new friends the Herberts and doing charity work, but, in truth, she knew she had resumed her old, pointless life. What was she to do?

She could still marry Richard Monckton Milnes. In June 1849, he pressed her for an answer to his proposal. He had been waiting seven years for her to make up her mind and had no desire to wait any longer. Yet Florence was still wavering. She was fond of Milnes—fonder of him than she cared to admit—but when she tried to say yes, the word caught in her throat. Writing helped her think, so on paper she weighed the advantages and drawbacks of a life with Milnes. He was a bright man with a warm heart, so the marriage would fulfill the intellectual and passionate sides of her nature, she knew. But what about her moral nature, her need to do great good? "I could not satisfy this nature by spending a life with him in making society and arranging domestic things," she wrote. "To be nailed to a continuation and exaggeration of my present life, without the hope of another, would be intolerable to me." It would seem, she thought, "like suicide." This one negative point outweighed all the pluses. She had to turn Milnes down.

Hilary Bonham Carter sketched Florence immersed in a book. Reading fed Florence's curious mind. It also helped her fill idle hours at home.

With her decision, Florence again threw the household into a tumult. Parthenope wailed, and Fanny Nightingale shouted. Flo was twenty-nine years old, and spinsterhood was fast approaching. By turning down Milnes, she might have given up her last chance for a secure place in the world. Suppose her father were to die in a carriage accident or from a disease? Through marriage, she might have produced a son — an heir to the Nightingale estate — and assured her mother and sister of a safe future. As it was, if anything happened to William Nightingale, all three women could be cast out of their homes with nowhere to turn.

Yes, yes; Florence had heard all the arguments before. She walked numbly from room to room. To her father, she looked like someone in shock.

CHAPTER 4

The Prison Called Family

A LETTER came from the Bracebridges—at the best possible moment. They were planning a journey to Egypt and Greece, and they were inviting Flo to come with them.

A trip to Egypt was nothing like a trip to Rome. Travelers to Egypt faced the dangers of a sea voyage while crossing the Mediterranean. Upon arriving, they endured intense heat and sandstorms. Gales were known to whip up violent waves on the broad, life-giving Nile River, putting boaters in peril. The river was home to crocodiles, and the desert harbored bandits. Disease was everywhere in Egypt; many Europeans got sick there, and some died.

For all these reasons, going to Egypt was far riskier than working at the Salisbury Infirmary. Yet "your letter of this morning makes everything so easy," Mrs. Nightingale responded to Selina Bracebridge. "If you will take our dear child, for better or worse," she wrote, "she shall be yours." Desperate for peace at home, Flo's parents gave their consent.

Despite the hazards, Egypt had become a popular destination for Europeans and Americans. They were lured by the tombs and monuments that Western

Tourists saw the Great Sphinx of Giza buried to its shoulders in sand when they visited Egypt in the mid-nineteenth century.

adventurers were discovering—and plundering—in this arid land. Tourists gazed in wonder at pyramids that were thousands of years old and at the strange hieroglyphics that adorned temple walls. Some hardy vacationers helped dig out the Great Sphinx, which was buried under centuries of drifting sand.

Florence thanked her family "a thousand times" for letting her go, telling them, "I hope I shall come back to be more of a comfort to you than ever I have been." Feeling a burst of renewed energy, she busily gathered the many things she would need while away, from parasols and practical linen dresses to books on modern and ancient Egypt. She bought a Levinge bed, a cloth sleeping sack with attached mosquito netting. She packed oil to rub on her skin to keep away the biting pests that swarmed along the banks of the Nile. On November 1, 1849, Florence and the Bracebridges left England. A grumpy German maid, Miss Trautwein, traveled with Florence this time. Florence called her Trout.

On the train that barreled across France to the Mediterranean, Florence met a pair of nursing nuns, members of the Sisters of Charity of St. Vincent de Paul. They gave her a letter of introduction that served her well in the first Egyptian city the group visited, Alexandria. After presenting this letter at the city's hospital, she was allowed to observe the sisters treating the sick from surrounding villages. "There are only nineteen of them, but they seem to do the work of ninety," Florence informed her family in England. Many poor Egyptians suffered from a severe diarrheal disease called dysentery or from painful eye infections that could lead to blindness. People contracted these ailments by drinking and washing in contaminated water. "Today I saw there a little orphan girl of nine years, who had found, some months ago, a deserted baby in the streets, and had adopted it," Florence wrote. "The baby is now ill, and the little foster-mother brings it daily to the convent for medicine."

Florence and the Bracebridges toured Alexandria, a leading seaport of the ancient world that was once home to a great library. In 1849 Alexandria was a city of narrow, crowded streets and flat-roofed houses. In late November, Florence and her fellow travelers boarded a steamship bound for their next destination, Cairo. Sailing on the same vessel was the great French writer Gustave Flaubert. He noticed some English travelers whom he took to be a family. They were "hideous," in his opinion. "The mother looks like a sick old parrot (because of the green eyeshade attached to her bonnet)," he wrote. Could this "family" have been Florence and her companions? Could the "mother" have been Selina Bracebridge?

Upon reaching Cairo, Charles Bracebridge hired a houseboat for cruising on the

Nile, as well as a staff of servants and a crew to navigate the river. The boat had sails, but on windless days the crew manned oars or walked along the bank, hauling the craft forward with ropes. The Bracebridges and Flo christened the boat *Parthenope*. It left port on December 4, flying the British flag and a blue and white pennant sewn by Florence that bore the name *Parthenope* stitched in Greek letters. The English travelers were to spend three and a half months on the Nile, sailing hundreds of miles upriver to Nubia (a region of southern Egypt and northern Sudan) and then back to Cairo again. Along the way they disembarked to see world-famous wonders up close, always with an Egyptian guide. Florence learned how to ride across the sand on a donkey.

Florence was in an exotic land thousands of miles from home, but she found it hard to shake off her gray mood. Egypt appeared colorless; the pyramids left her cold; Trout got on her nerves. The two women quarreled at one tomb they visited when the cross servant sat and crocheted instead of looking at the scarabs and gods painted on the walls. "Dreadful fights with Trout," Florence jotted in her diary one day. In another entry, she noted a daytime "row with Trout . . . but luckily she had a tooth ache so I was spared saying anything that night."

Mostly, though, she spent days in "a sort of torpor," Florence wrote.

Their leisurely cruise on the Nile River offered Florence and the Bracebridges spectacular views of ancient monuments.

As she lay on the houseboat's divan and read aloud to her companions, her worries pressed on her. The same concerns kept running through her mind: her ambitions, her family's expectations, and the impossibility of satisfying both. She began to doubt herself, to think that God had never really called her, that it all had been a mistake. At last, in March, as she walked in a village, she sensed that He communicated with her again. Florence believed that she heard Madre Santa Colomba, far away in Italy, affirming that God had chosen Florence to follow a singular path. She wrote in her diary, "God called me with my Madre's words." But if God had spoken once more, He offered no solution to the problem of living her life.

Florence showed her brighter side in the many letters she sent to her family at home. Egypt, she wrote, was "a country which, like its own old Nile, has overflowed and fertilized the world." She wrote vividly about Cairo, "the latticed windows meeting overhead, the pearls of Moorish architecture at every corner, the looking up to the blue sky and golden sunlight from the wells of streets and in the bazaars." She described the Nile, which was "beautiful, beautiful, though one can hardly tell why." To Florence the Nile was a living thing, "like a great sea, he is so wide—and when the wind freshens, you see a fleet of little cangias [sailboats] coming out, like water-lilies." She discussed ancient and modern faiths, stating that she found "much good in the Mahometan religion [Islam]. Charity is unbounded; and it is not the charity of patronage, but the charity of fellowship."

Such fine letters needed to be shared. Flo's parents and sister read them to friends and relatives. And as everyone marveled at the extraordinary things Florence had done and seen, Parthenope grew ill. She appeared to be ailing in both body and mind. Her parents sent her to stay with family friends in London, hoping a change of scene might do their older daughter some good.

Meanwhile, in April, Florence and the others reached Athens, Greece, where the Bracebridges had a house. Florence was still depressed. The famous ruins of Athens—the columns and steps of once-majestic temples to the gods—were smaller than she had imagined them. The whole place looked like "a cork model," she said.

One day, outside the Parthenon, the temple of the goddess Athena, Florence spotted some children teasing a baby owl that had fallen from its nest. She hurried over and convinced the youngsters to sell her the little bird, which was nothing more than a tiny ball of fluff. The owl, which Florence called Athena, became her cherished pet. Florence fed her by hand and taught her to sit on a finger or in a pocket. Selina Bracebridge sewed a cloth sack that was just the right size for Athena, one that closed with a drawstring loosely around the owlet's neck. Bundled cozily, Athena liked to sleep on Florence's lap. But even with Athena bringing her joy, Florence stayed awake at night, worrying about her direction in life. She declared herself "physically & morally ill & broken down, a slave."

The Parthenon was in ruins for centuries. A major restoration project began in 1984.

On May 12, Florence turned thirty, the age when "Christ began his mission," as she wrote in her diary. For herself this birthday marked a turning point: "No more childish things, no more vain things, no more love, no more marriage." From this moment on, her life would have a single purpose: "O Lord, Thy will, Thy will."

In June, Florence and the Bracebridges left Greece for home, a trip that took them through Germany. After watching Florence spend a week in Berlin feeling miserable, Selina Bracebridge stepped in, knowing just what her young friend needed. If Flo wanted to spend two weeks at the nursing institute at Kaiserswerth, Mrs. Bracebridge and her husband would wait for her in nearby Düsseldorf. For Florence, going to Kaiserswerth was the answer to many prayers. There was no time to seek her parents' permission, so she would go without it. And she left Trout behind; she could learn to style her own hair.

The deaconesses who trained at Kaiserswerth belonged to a Protestant sisterhood that served God through charitable work. The institute where they studied and practiced had been founded in 1836 by Pastor Theodor Fliedner, a Lutheran minister. It maintained an orphanage, schools, and a home for women prisoners returning to society. Its hospital held more than a hundred beds arranged in wards for men, women, and children. A seasoned, qualified nurse taught the deaconesses how to perform such tasks as dressing wounds, bathing the sick, and placing sharp-smelling plasters on patients' chests to treat pneumonia. The women also learned to prepare medicines and lay out the dead. Because theirs was a religious calling, the deaconesses took part in Bible readings on the wards every morning and night. They were required to be clean, orderly, hard-working, obedient, and sober.

Florence introduced herself to Fliedner and his wife and was thrilled to be admitted to the institute. Once inside, she toured the hospital wards and observed the

Pastor Theodor Fliedner founded the institute at Kaiserswerth in 1836. In 1850 he asked Florence Nightingale to write a pamphlet about the school.

teachers at work in the schools. She went on night rounds with the apothecary. One day, she tagged along as some of the deaconesses brought children to bathe in the Rhine River. She joined the deaconesses for their simple meals, usually vegetable soup. (They ate meat just twice a week.) She felt at home in this friendly place where everyone shared equally.

No one can become a trained nurse in two weeks. The deaconesses spent at least two years learning their craft. Still, after her stay at Kaiserswerth, Florence felt invincible, "as if nothing could ever vex me again," she said. Pastor Fliedner asked her to write a brochure about the institute to inform other English people about its important work. She spent five days drafting a thirty-two-page pamphlet. In it she did more than describe the institute and its work, as Fliedner had requested. She also traced the tradition of nursing the sick to the "very first times of Christianity," when it allowed for "the employment of woman's powers directly in the service of GOD."

In her own day, she wrote, nursing might offer unmarried women a chance to do meaningful work. Well-to-do ladies often made charitable visits to the poor, and Nightingale had done this herself. Yet women left these visits feeling useless. Nightingale wrote, "We say to ourselves, 'But what good do I do? I ask the mother, how many children go to school? — perhaps I preach a little; I give a little book and a blanket. . . . I see illness, but I do not know how to manage it, and yet that would be the very thing I should like to do.'" About these frustrated women, she asked, "What are they to do with that thirst for action, useful action, which every woman feels?"

After nearly nine months away from home, the English travelers reached London on the night of August 20. The next morning, Florence said goodbye to Selina and Charles Bracebridge and boarded a train to Lea Hurst. Within hours she sat in the drawing room of the house she loved, surrounded by a family happy to have her back. They were doubly delighted when Athena popped out of Flo's pocket to greet them.

Soon, all the Nightingales doted on Athena. "If an armchair was drawn up to the fire, she always considered that it was done for her especial use," Parthenope wrote. "Placing herself exactly in the middle she would comfortably shut one eye draw up one leg & wink luxuriously and magnificently at the fire for an hour at a time." Athena was known to be a thief. More than once, the sisters found fur cuffs that had been missing for months in the out-of-the-way places where Athena had stashed them. "To have knocked down a jar of roses and carried off the finest to the top of the room was a feat which greatly delighted her," Parthe said.

The family learned to understand Athena's calls: "a bark when she was naughty, a crow when she was proud, a little purr (a sort of twee twee) when she was pleased, a grumble when she was cross & a hoot when she was melancholy," Parthe explained. "She would go on talking sometimes the whole morning, always putting in an observation when a pause in the reading, or an enquiring tone seemed to require it."

Despite the joy Athena brought, the old anger and frustration soon resurfaced in the Nightingale household. Flo's parents disapproved of her stay at Kaiserswerth. Things were going to be different now that she was back in England, they said. If she wanted to help people, then she could visit the poor of the parish. If she wanted to

Parthenope drew this picture of Florence and the much-loved Athena.

nurse someone, she could tend to her sister. In fact, Mrs. Nightingale decided, for the next six months, Flo was to devote herself entirely to Parthe's care.

It was an idea that could never work. If Flo tried to help her sister, Parthe pulled away. If Flo spoke, Parthe whined that her voice sounded like a trumpet and gave her indigestion. "I can hardly open my mouth without giving my dear Parthe vexation," Flo griped. There was no way for Flo to win, for if she kept silent, then Parthe complained that she was too quiet. Parthe accused Flo of caring more about the people in the village than her own family and of still planning to train as a nurse.

Instead of encouraging peace and cooperation, Mrs. Nightingale took Parthe's side and lectured Flo. Mr. Nightingale, as usual, refused to support Fanny and Parthe or stand up for Flo. "My selfishness tells me to let all alone & leave you womenfolk to your own battles" was all he would say.

Florence once described Parthenope as someone who was at peace being a mid-nineteenth-century Englishwoman. But Parthe's behavior signaled that her real feelings were different. As a child Parthe had heard her mother praise Florence to their governess. In her teens she had seen her younger sister excel at difficult studies with their father. She had been the one left out when Flo and their cousins amused themselves at the piano. She had stayed home while Flo went off on two exciting adventures, to Rome and then to Egypt and Greece. And she had stood by as Flo rejected a marriage proposal from a worthy man while in all this time, no suitors had ever called on her. For Parthenope to resent Florence was only natural. Parthe, like Florence, was stuck in the role of an unmarried woman, a grown-up daughter in her parents' home. She felt the same social constraints that Florence did, but she lacked Florence's great ambition — Florence's possible way out.

It was a dreary time for both sisters. Word reached England that Henry Nicholson, the cousin who had taught Flo algebra, had died in a carriage accident in Spain. No one knew exactly how this tragedy had happened. According to one witness, the carriage, with seventeen passengers, had tumbled over a cliff and fallen into the sea. Another claimed that a giant wave had suddenly washed the vehicle away. It hardly mattered which story was true; in either case, Henry was gone. Trying to accept Henry's death as "God's will," Florence spent a week at Waverley with the grieving Nicholsons. She comforted her aunt Anne, who dwelled on the twists of fate that had brought Henry to the place where he died. "The poor mother cannot quite keep 'if this' and 'if that had not been so' out of her mind's eye," Florence observed. Her uncle George could barely say a word, and her cousin Marianne cried wildly. "Her path is a hard one," Florence noted.

Around this time Florence saw Richard Monckton Milnes at a party, and her face briefly brightened. She expected him to greet her warmly, as an old friend, but "he would hardly speak. I was miserable," she said. "He did not show indifference, but avoidance. No familiar friendship. No confidence such as I felt towards him." A few weeks later, Milnes announced his engagement to someone else.

Sadness, disappointment, and strife. Florence sank so low that she was nearly suicidal. "I feel myself perishing when I go to bed," she announced dramatically at Christmas in 1850. "I have no desire now but to die."

The fighting in the Nightingale home worsened in 1851 after Charles Bracebridge arranged for Florence's small book on Kaiserswerth to be printed. *The Institution of Kaiserswerth on the Rhine: For the Practical Training of Deaconesses* was published anonymously, but some of the family's acquaintances guessed who its author was. "People seem to understand that Flo wrote the little Kaiserswerth pamphlet," Aunt Patty informed Mrs. Nightingale, who was far from pleased.

Helping Liz Herbert with the birth of her third child allowed Flo a brief escape from what she termed "the prison which is called a family." The doctor tending to Herbert was Elizabeth Blackwell, the world's first licensed female physician. Blackwell was born in England in 1821 but moved with her family to the United States when she was eleven years old. She was fortunate to have open-minded parents who supported her dream of being a doctor. In 1847, she became the only female student at Geneva Medical College (now Hobart College) in New York State. The faculty members reviewing her application preferred not to accept a woman but could find no valid reason to turn down a qualified candidate. They asked the students to decide, and the all-male student body, thinking it was a joke, voted to admit her. The professors and students expected her to fail, but she graduated first in her class in 1849. Blackwell continued her studies in Paris at La Maternité, a maternity, or lying-in, hospital, where the administrators denied her equal status with the male physicians.

When Nightingale met her, Blackwell was doing further study in London. She would struggle for acceptance in a man's profession at every step in her career. Yet she felt proud that she could support herself.

Blackwell was a small woman whose fair hair shone red and golden in sunlight. On April 17, 1851, she visited her friend Florence at Embley. It was a perfect day; "the laurels were in full bloom," Blackwell remembered. The two women strolled the grounds, admiring the house and gardens. As they paused outside the drawing room, Nightingale said, "Do you know what I always think when I look at that row of windows? I think how I should turn it into a hospital ward, and just how I should place the beds!" Two weeks later, Nightingale spent a day with Blackwell in London. The women toured a hospital for patients with spinal problems and heard a lecture on political economy. After dining with the Bracebridges, they parted with tears, only to meet again on June 23. On that day they toured the German Hospital in northeast London. Employing nurses trained at Kaiserswerth, this hospital served the city's many poor German immigrants. Nightingale and Blackwell signed their names in the hospital's visitors' book and parted again.

Elizabeth Blackwell defied the expectations of her teachers and fellow students and in 1849 became the first woman to graduate from a medical school.

Florence Nightingale admired Elizabeth Blackwell but had no desire to be a doctor herself. She believed medicine ought to remain a man's realm, with nursing—a womanly profession—standing apart from it. Nurses focused on cleanliness and comfort. They did more than doctors to help patients recover, Nightingale thought. Doctors could prescribe treatments and potions, but "medicine does not cure," she would one day claim. "It is Nature only that cures."

Could nature cure her sister's distress? Their parents thought so. They felt Parthe might benefit from the mineral waters available at German spas. And, they announced, in a complete about-face, while nature was helping her sister recover, Flo could spend three months at the institute at Kaiserswerth.

CHAPTER 5

Shadows in a Thirsty Land

WHAT had changed?

For five years, Flo's parents had stubbornly opposed her nursing plans. They had stood solidly on widely held beliefs about proper occupations for women. Then, in 1851, they found themselves on shifting ground. "Young ladies of a standing in society, quite equal to Flo's, do things *now* of this kind, which were unheard of formerly," Selina Bracebridge told Mrs. Nightingale. "They are not in any way looked down upon because they devote themselves to Hospitals or Patients."

What Selina said was true. Pastor Fliedner's influence was spreading beyond Germany. In England, the Sisters of St. John's House, an Anglican nursing order, had been founded in 1848. These women trained in London and cared for the sick in hospitals and homes. Deaconesses from Kaiserswerth staffed London's German Hospital, as Flo had observed. And they were taking their skills to other European countries and to the United States.

Flo's parents worried about her state of mind, and those concerns might have contributed to their change of heart as well. She had spoken of her wish to die; would she go so far as to take her own life? Mr. Nightingale had come to see that Florence needed "some great absorption." Perhaps he and his wife would be wise to let her explore nursing further.

That summer, Flo journeyed to Carlsbad, a German-speaking town in what is now the Czech Republic, with her mother, her sister, and Athena. Famed for its hot springs, Carlsbad today is called Karlovy Vary. From there Flo would go on to Kaiserswerth while Parthe stayed and sought benefits from Carlsbad's alkaline springs. People hoping for cures came to this picturesque valley to drink the water, sometimes downing forty glasses of it in a single day. They also bathed in it "in order that the water should bite into the skin and thereby allow the unwholesome matter and detrimental fluids to flow away," as one guidebook explained.

Hot, bubbling, purportedly health-giving water gushes from a fountain at Carlsbad.

Mrs. Nightingale was trying hard to accept Flo's ambition. Even so, she insisted that Flo's stay at the institute be kept secret from their family and friends in England. Flo replied that secrecy was useless. The Bracebridges knew what she was doing and so did Aunt Mai. Mai had told her son, Shore, who had praised his cousin's pluck. It was just a matter of time till others found out.

Parthe grew more and more upset as Flo's departure neared. On the night before Flo was to leave, Parthe let her fury fly. The sisters had a terrible fight, hurling cruel accusations back and forth. When she ran out of words, Parthe pulled off her bracelets—presents Flo had brought her from Egypt—and flung them in her sister's face. Flo felt so distressed that she fainted.

Putting her thoughts on paper, Florence noted with frustration, "Everything that I have to do that concerns my real being must be done with a struggle." She asked, "Why, oh my God, cannot I be satisfied with the life which satisfies so many people?"

Things improved greatly for Florence on July 6, 1851, when she donned the blue uniform of a Kaiserswerth deaconess. She worked in all sections of the institute, including the children's ward. At times she sat with the dying and helped them through the night. One man faded quietly into death while she read to him. "When he was gone, I sat on the window sill and looked out on the busy, lighted town," she wrote. "Death is so much more impressive in the midst of life."

On the morning of July 31, she assisted surgeons who were amputating a man's leg. A wound in the patient's leg was badly infected, and the only way to stop the infection from spreading was to cut off the limb. "Taking up of the arteries beautiful. Sawing of the bone momentary," Nightingale jotted in her notes. The surgery appeared successful. Afterward, nurses applied cold-water compresses to the amputation site every five minutes to ease the patient's pain and reduce swelling. "One of us

Florence fulfilled a long-held dream when she stepped through the doors of the Deaconess Institute at Kaiserswerth.

always with him," Nightingale wrote. For several days, the patient improved. Then he showed signs of infection and sank into unconsciousness. The day after that, he died.

Nightingale paid close attention to how the female superintendent ran the hospital. "She has to consider herself as the mother of the house," Nightingale wrote, "& cares for it with zeal & love & power." Nightingale saw that all the sisters obeyed the superintendent, that they gave her "an account of their office & have to take her counsel thereupon." The superintendent conferred often with Pastor Fliedner. "Once a week she gives an account to the Pastor of the spiritual state of the sick," Nightingale noted.

While at the institute, Florence received a sincere, loving letter from her mother. Fanny Nightingale had had a change of heart and had written things that were

Deaconesses care for the young in the children's sickroom at Kaiserswerth.

too hard for her to say in person. "You yourself cannot have been more thankful to Kaiserswerth than we all have been at this time, as a shadow in a thirsty land for you," Mrs. Nightingale wrote. "Yes, my dear, take time, take faith & love with you, even though it be to walk in a path which leads you strangely from us all." She vowed, "We will do our best to have faith as you ask."

Parthe's letters were different, full of complaints. She was still unwell, the summer was too hot, and she was having no fun. And somehow it was all Flo's fault. She was sick and tired of Florence and her ambition.

Hoping Parthenope might yet accept her for who she was, Florence penned a patient reply. "My earnest affection, my heartfelt gratitude are yours, but I have also thirst for what I believe to be my right work," she wrote. "Your blessing on my following my sense of right in my path of life is what I most desire." Parthe was too angry, though, to consider what Flo had to say.

After the Nightingales returned to England, it seemed that Flo was hardly ever home. When her father developed an eye ailment in early 1852, she went with him to Umberslade Park, in west-central England, to be treated by a Dr. Johnson. This practitioner struck Florence as "a little, strange, scrubby, boorish-looking man," yet he was also "the most careful, impartial, disinterested, clever water doctor I have known." Johnson dispensed a popular treatment known as the cold-water cure. His patients endured a regimen of cold showers, brisk walks, and healthy meals to stimulate their circulation and make them well.

Mr. Nightingale especially liked the food in Umberslade. "Papa says capital mutton & potatoes, beautiful brown bread pudding & today a beautiful apple Charlotte," Florence informed her mother. In his own letters home, William Nightingale reported "no grievances — plenty of fires — good rooms." Flo, he said, "is a good right hand & is quite full of work & preparation." After a month his eyes had improved enough for him to go home, although they would give him trouble for years to come.

Florence then spent much of the spring with Aunt Mai. The two women took a train to the walled city of York to see its famed cathedral, York Minster. In July they called on a writer named Mary Ann Evans. Six months older than Florence, Evans worked for the *Westminster Review*, a liberal journal, and was living in the London home of its editor in chief, John Chapman. This unconventional household also included Chapman's wife, his children, and his mistress. Evans was his assistant, but she did all the actual work while he enjoyed the credit. She would later gain fame as the author of *Middlemarch* and other important Victorian novels, which she published under the pen name George Eliot.

Evans told a friend that she admired Mai Smith's "freedom and simplicity." About Miss Florence Nightingale, she said, "I was much pleased with her. There is a loftiness of mind about her which is well expressed by her form and manners."

By this time, any improvement Parthenope had enjoyed after her stay in Carlsbad had vanished. Parthe was in an alarming state, complaining of headaches, having hysterical outbursts, and making life impossible for her parents. She insisted that she was dying and

Under the pen name George Eliot, Mary Ann Evans published her first novel, *Adam Bede*, in 1859.

that Florence's activities were killing her. Mr. and Mrs. Nightingale were desperate. They called in one of England's finest medical men, Sir James Clark, who was Queen Victoria's personal physician. Upon examining Parthe, Clark found a patient who was "nervous, fanciful, and unstable." He sensed that her problems were more than physical; something about her way of life was making them worse. Sending her away from home, he advised her parents, offered Parthe the best chance of recovery. For this reason, he took her to Birkhall, an estate in Scotland owned by the royal family where the Clarks were currently living. Sir James believed in the benefits of clean, fresh air. He wanted Parthe to hike in the hilly Highlands, far from her mother's coddling.

With Parthe away in Scotland, Florence went to Ireland with the Nightingales' friends the Fowlers—the doctor in charge of the Salisbury Infirmary and his wife. This older couple was attending some meetings in Belfast, and Florence hoped to tour Irish hospitals. The trip proved disappointing, though. St. Vincent's Hospital in Dublin, which Florence had especially hoped to see, was closed for repairs. And Belfast, to her, was "about as unspiritual and uninteresting as it is possible to conceive."

The travelers made their way back to Dublin, where they were to board a ferry for England, and found a letter waiting there for Florence. It was from Charlotte Clark, Sir James's daughter. In it Florence read that Parthenope was worse than ever and was demanding that Florence come to her right away. "She has a great longing for you," Charlotte Clark wrote.

Wasting no time, Florence caught a boat bound for Scotland and reached Birkhall on September 13. She found Parthe plagued by fantasies and fears. "The flood whirls about my head," Parthe said. Sir James was convinced that Parthe's illness was purely emotional. He diagnosed "absolutely no disease but a marked irritability of the brain." As Flo told her mother, "Sir James says, if she could but think herself well she would be so, or rather if she could but think of something else." Speaking confidentially, the good doctor said that Florence's presence in the home upset Parthenope's fragile mental balance. It would be best if Florence lived apart from the rest of the family.

Florence knew all too well that she caused much of Parthe's distress, but she also knew that it made no difference where she was, at home or away. Simply the idea of Florence and the life she had chosen was enough to send Parthe into a frenzy. Florence felt like "a stranded ship," she wrote to a friend. For the moment, though, Parthe seemed satisfied that she had made Florence come all the way to Scotland, and she settled down.

As soon as Parthe felt well enough, Florence took her to Lea Hurst. They made the rail journey slowly, going only as far each day as Parthe, in her illness, could handle. At their second stop, Edinburgh, Parthe insisted she was too weak to climb into the railway carriage by herself and had a porter carry her.

Once home, Parthe sent a long, cranky letter to the sisters' old friend Clarkey, listing all Florence's faults. Flo "has little or none of what is called charity or philanthropy, she is ambitious—very, and would like very well

Birkhall was built in 1715 and acquired by the royal family in 1849. Today it is a private residence of Prince Charles, the heir to the British throne.

to regenerate the world," Parthe complained. "Here she has a circle of admirers who cry up everything she does or says as gospel." Parthe thought Flo would benefit from spending time with Clarkey, since, "though you love and admire her, [you] do not believe in the wisdom of all she does or says, *because* SHE says it." Clarkey reminded

Parthe of the need to respect individual differences. She pointed out, "Flo you know has more of activity and hunger for discovery than the mere want of doing good."

Mai Smith and Selina Bracebridge also had opinions about Flo, and they shared them with each other and with Fanny Nightingale. Smith thought Flo needed to put into practice "these ideas, so busy working within." Bracebridge thought Flo's father should provide her with an income and let her live independently. It was the least he could do "for having a child of such *power* & genius."

Mr. and Mrs. Nightingale listened. When an aged aunt of William Nightingale's died in December 1852, they proposed that Flo use her house in Derbyshire, near the spot where the peaceful river Derwent flowed under the Cromford Bridge, for the nursing sisterhood she had once dreamed of forming. Flo thanked them, but she turned the offer down. She was not yet ready to start a sisterhood, she said. She wanted to go to Paris for more training with the Sisters of Charity, a Roman Catholic nursing order. Mrs. Nightingale hesitated, but at last she gave her consent.

Paris had been a grieving city when the Nightingales went there in 1838. In January 1853, it was sparkling and spirited. Napoleon III, France's self-proclaimed emperor, was soon to marry a beautiful Spanish countess. Notre Dame, Paris's great Gothic cathedral, looked like "an old actress at a fair, painted and dressed up in old finery," Flo wrote to her mother. "She is all gaudied out with flags and hangings and old draperies." Flo spent her first two weeks in Paris with Clarkey and her husband, Julius Mohl. Fanny was pleased to hear that Flo had attended two balls and several parties. Julius Mohl obtained a government permit that allowed Florence to tour the Hôpital des Enfants Malades, the world's first institute for sick children, and other Parisian hospitals. She visited wards, observed operations, and gathered reports that she could hardly wait to analyze.

It was mid-February when she entered the Maison de la Providence, the hospital run by the Sisters of Charity. She nursed the sick under the sisters' guidance, but she had barely begun her work when she received word that her grandmother Shore was deathly ill. She immediately returned to England because no one in the family knew more than she did about nursing the dying.

In the old house where, twenty-seven years before, she had eaten cake at Mai and Sam Smith's wedding breakfast, she found the old woman confused, bedridden, and failing. "The first snowdrops are come, but she will not live to see them," Florence knew. When her father came to be with his mother for the last time, Florence darkened the room to keep him from seeing how withered she was. Grandmother Shore suffered through a nightmarish final week, struggling to breathe and crying out in pain. "She bears it like a hero," Florence said. Just after the woman died, Florence composed a tender letter to her father: "I hope the sun shines on you, dear Papa. The full moon shone on the waste of snow last night, as the face grew beautiful in the light of death and young in the hope of life."

"Great had been the occasion for her usefulness, great the comfort she had administered," Mr. Nightingale said of Florence. It brought him peace to know that Florence had held his mother's hands "till the last of her moments on earth." The only consolation Florence had asked for herself was to have Athena brought to her. "I shall want her company after this," she said.

Grandmother Shore died on March 25; on April 18, Florence was in London to call on Lady Charlotte Canning. Lady Canning was on a women's committee that governed a small charity hospital. The committee was looking for a new superintendent, and Selina Bracebridge had recommended Florence Nightingale.

The Establishment for Gentlewomen During Illness cared for refined, educated ladies who had no money or loved ones to nurse them. Some had been governesses; others were the widows, daughters, and nieces of clergymen and military officers. As a guidebook to London charities explained, these ladies were "prevented by their position from entering the hospitals." In too many cases, "delicacy and the feeling of independence" kept them from turning to others for help. As a result, they often passed "from temporary illness into premature and hopeless decay, for want of that relief which this establishment proposes to afford."

Canning was surprised by Nightingale's youth—the candidate was not quite thirty-three—and her mettle. The woman who sat before her had never been in charge of an institution, yet she felt no shyness about negotiating. She would

A mother brings her children to meet their new governess. A governess occupied a difficult position in English society. She was an educated woman from the family of a clergyman, military officer, or poor aristocrat, which made her the social equal of her employer. Yet by working for money she lowered herself to the level of a servant. Such a woman had no resources to fall back on if she became ill.

take the job only if she could run the hospital as she thought best, Nightingale said. She wanted to watch when surgery was being performed. She also wanted to listen in as doctors spoke with patients, so she could be sure the nursing staff carried out medical instructions. When it was her turn to lay out terms, Canning said that Nightingale would have to live at the institution. She would be paid no salary—no lady of means worked for money. And she would have to bring a servant, whose wages Flo would pay herself, to be her housekeeper and chaperone.

The committee offered Florence the position, and she took it.

Mr. Nightingale gave Florence a yearly allowance of five hundred pounds, enough to ensure her independence. He also gave her advice about managing the hospital, although he had never worked a day in his life. He counseled her to heed suggestions from the nurses she supervised, to govern her institution "by a representative system." As he explained, "Despots do nothing in teaching others." Then he hurried off to his club so he would be away from home when Parthenope heard the news. "Parthe can no more control or moderate the intensity of her interest in Flo's doings than she can change her physical form," he believed. He considered sending Parthe away, thinking that "her life will be sacrificed to the activity of her thoughts unless she removes herself immediately from the scene." But he changed his mind, deciding that sending her away "might do more harm than good." He had no idea how to help Parthenope.

CHAPTER 6

"But One Person in England"

ELIZABETH Blackwell wrote from New York to congratulate Nightingale on her new job. "I look upon your position as a very noble one, weakening the barriers of prejudice which hedge in all *work* for women," Blackwell told her English friend.

By taking charge of a small hospital, Nightingale may well have been clearing the way for women who wanted careers, but she needed to focus on the task at hand. She hired a housekeeper named Mary Clarke (who was not related to Mary Clarke Mohl, Nightingale's friend Clarkey). By mid-July 1853, Nightingale was overseeing the Establishment for Gentlewomen During Illness as it moved into a freshly renovated house on Upper Harley Street.

So much needed to be done! The place was dusty, and the hospital's linens were torn and ragged. She had maids clean the house from top to bottom. Mary Clarke and two seamstresses mended anything they could. They pushed their needles through yard after yard of cotton, making new pillowcases, tablecloths, and towels. When it was time to move patients in, workers were still installing dumbwaiters to carry food and supplies from floor to floor, and bells for patients to use when calling a nurse.

(1)   Disease   Admitted 5 January 1853

Ovarian Dropsy   Mrs. Parez
Complicated with Ascites   age 60

{ Dr. Farre & Dr. Pierce Jones
{ Mr. Bowman

6   Decoct. Genista   ℨxv
       Sp. Juniperi   ℨi   m.
    take 3 tablespoonful 3 times
    a day
       Manna Opt.   ℨiv

8   Liq. Chl. Calcis   ℨviij
        Prison
    a tablespoonful to 1 pt water
    for Injection.

11   Liq. Ammon. Acet.   ℨij
    Sp. Eth. nitri   ℨiij
    Syr. Papav. alb   ℨss
    Tra Camphor. C   ℨiiss
    Mist. Campt.   ad.   ℨvi

22   Unguent. Sodinii comp. ℨi

    Zinci Sulph.   ℨss
    Aluminis   ℨss
    ⅓ of each in cold water
    as a lotion renewed every
    4 days & bathe the Prolapsus
    Ani with every morning with
    a sponge –
    afterwards prop it up with
    the Sponge & put the strap
    over it.

Feb 1   Rep. Mistura Etheris &c
    ℞ Sp. Ether. Sulphur. Co. ℨij

    Ammon. Sesq. Carb.   gr x
    Soda Sesq. Carb.   gr xx
    Tr Sumbuli   ℨiss
    Sp. Ether. Sulph. Co.   ℨss
    Aq. Camphora   ad   ℨiv
    the fourth part every three or
    four hours if necessary

5   Decoct. Scoparii   ad   ℨvi
    Sp. ether. nitri   ℨiij
    Tinct. Scilla   ℨi
    Tinct. camph. comp.   ℨiij
    Syrup. tolu   ℨvi
    ft. mist.
    take two tablespoonful
    every six hours

Feb 15   Ammon. Sesq. Carb.   gr xvi
    Tr. Cinchona Co.   ℨiv
    – Sumbuli   ℨiss
    Sp. Etheris Co.   ℨiss
    – Armoracia C.   ℨi
    Aq. Camphora   ad   ℨiv
    fourth part every 3 or 4 hours
    if necessary

17   Sp. Ether. Nitri   ℨiv
    Ammon. Sesquicarb.   ℨss
    Sp. Juniperi comp.   ℨvi
    Tr. Lavandula Co.   ℨiij
    Mist. Camphora   ad   ℨvi
    ft. mistura. take two table
    spoonful every four hours

18   Hydrarg. Chlorid.   gr ij
    Opii   gr ¼
    pill to be taken every 6 hours
    Blister to be put on the right
    side

23   Strong Peppermint Lozenges ℨi

    Cerat. Sabina
        Cantharidis   āā   ℨss
    misce

24   Oxid. Zinci   ℨi

March 4   Sp. Etheris Nitri.   ℨi
    Potassa Nitri.   ℨi
    Tr. Lyttae   ℨiii
    Sp. Junip. C.   ℨi
    Aqua Cinnamomi   ad   ℨxii
    take 3 tablespoonful every 4 hours

6   Ammon. Sesquisalic   ℨss
    Moraciis   ℈i
    Mist. Camphora   ℨvi
    ft. mist.
    take fourth part every 6 hours

A page from Florence Nightingale's Harley Street casebook. Nightingale kept a careful record of every medication and treatment administered to the women under her care.

Nightingale soon was doing things she had never imagined she would do, such as haggling with butchers and stopping drunken workmen from fighting.

The house held beds for twenty-seven patients. Two rooms had been set aside as the superintendent's quarters, but Nightingale also leased a flat outside the hospital for those times when she needed to get away.

Superintendent Nightingale found small ways to cut costs. Even having the kitchen maids make jam instead of buying it saved needed pounds. She replaced careless staff with people who worked hard and well. She "changed one housemaid, on account of her love of dirt and inexperience, and one nurse, on account of her love of opium," she said. She also stood up to the ladies' committee when she learned that they refused to admit Roman Catholic patients.

Catholics had faced persecution in England since 1534, when King Henry VIII broke ties with the Vatican and established the Church of England. Henry had seized Catholic monasteries and convents throughout his kingdom and confiscated their wealth. Until 1778, it was against the law in England for Catholics to buy or inherit land, join the army, or worship freely. Before 1829, they were barred from holding public office. Many English Protestants still had anti-Catholic attitudes in the 1850s.

Nightingale insisted that women of all faiths should be cared for in her hospital and that their clergymen should be allowed to visit them. She threatened to resign immediately unless the restriction was lifted. The committee gave in, but Nightingale had to promise in writing that she would escort visiting Catholic priests to patients' rooms and make sure they spoke to no one else.

The patients' ailments ranged from cancer to arthritis to scrofula—a tuberculosis infection that settled in the lymph nodes. Some patients had no hope of getting well, so the nurses made them comfortable in their final weeks of life. One day, a governess was brought in with severe mental illness. After she ran out into the street and caused a commotion, Nightingale had her transferred to St. Luke's Hospital for Lunatics. The mentally ill were poorly understood in the nineteenth century and often received cruel treatment in hospitals. They were frequently locked away from their families and friends, forced to endure torturous procedures, and allowed to talk to no one. St. Luke's might have been more humane, but even there, patients were plunged into cold baths and given medicines to make them vomit. Nightingale was unequipped to care for the unfortunate governess, though, and had no choice but to send her away.

St. Luke's Hospital was a dismal place where the mentally ill received little help.

Some of the women who claimed to be sick were in reality lonely, sad, or down on their luck. Nightingale was known to help them move on with gifts of cash and letters of recommendation that might get them hired as governesses. Many nights, she rubbed warmth into a patient's cold feet. These small acts of kindness made her popular with the women she cared for. She was the hospital's "sunshine," one said. Nightingale was doing the work that she believed God had called her to do, and she relished her independence.

Her parents sent her fruit and vegetables as well as game birds shot on the grounds at Embley. These gifts of food were a simple, wordless way to show their support. Even Parthenope was trying to accept the new Florence and had helped her decorate her rooms in the Upper Harley Street house. Parthe disapproved, though, of Flo's liberated ways. She was shocked—and she told Flo so—to hear that her sister walked to Covent Garden, London's big produce market, and shopped there like a servant. Defending her actions, Flo said, "You foolish child, don't you see that the Covent Garden expeditions are just the best thing I could do? They get me out— they give me air, exercise, variety."

As her year as superintendent came to a close, Nightingale informed the ladies' committee that she was resigning. The hospital was running smoothly, and she needed a bigger challenge. Lady Canning responded, "We well know that the great work you have always had at heart, namely, to improve hospital nursing, cannot be carried in such an institution as this." Canning continued, "We hope that the order and system you have established may enable another lady superintendent to carry in the institution with some degree of success, though we are without the slightest hope of meeting with your equal."

Nightingale left her post in August 1854, just as cholera was showing up in a

The bounty of England's farms was displayed for purchase at the Covent Garden market.

crowded section of London. This killer disease came on suddenly. A person might feel fine one day and be overcome by severe vomiting and watery diarrhea the next. The person's eyes looked sunken, and the skin grew gray, loose, and clammy. Other signs of dehydration were more ominous: a weak, rapid pulse, a struggle to breathe, and seizures. Death often followed quickly. Cholera sent its victim "to the vast abyss of eternity, to the presence of his Maker, almost before he has recovered from the first surprise of his attack," as one doctor dramatically put it. Before long, this outbreak grew into the worst one London had yet seen. One hundred and twenty-seven people died in the first three days of September. A week later, the death toll had reached five hundred.

"How is the cholera generated;—how spread. . . . These questions are in every mouth," stated an article in a London medical journal. "One moment warm, palpitating, human organisms—the next a sort of galvanized corpses, with icy breath, stopped pulse, and blood congealed—blue, shriveled up, convulsed." The cause of cholera "will probably ever remain, among the inscrutable secrets of nature," this writer concluded. It belonged "to a class of questions radically inaccessible to the human intelligence."

Doctors and scientists had come up with theories to explain cholera. According to the animalcular theory, "microscopic insects" invaded the body, causing disease. Some experts preferred the fungoid theory, which attributed cholera to an unknown fungus. There was also a telluric theory, which blamed a poison rising from the earth, and an electric theory, which pointed to "fluctuations of the atmospheric electricity." Additionally, the ozonic theory stated that cholera arose when there was too little ozone in the atmosphere.

Many people, including Florence Nightingale, accepted the miasma theory to explain disease. They believed that foul air released by rotting vegetable matter, dead animals, or decomposing corpses caused people to get sick. This deadly air, or miasma, could even arise from stagnant water. "The poison may be wafted east and west, north and south, on the winds of heaven, on the garments of the passerby," warned Dr. Edward T. Roe of the board of health in Plymouth, England. The best way to keep people well and help the sick recover was through sanitation, Roe and others taught. They called for better ventilation to bring "fresh air in the place of the deadly poison passing from the bodies of the dying."

Nightingale volunteered at London's Middlesex Hospital, where she supervised the care of cholera victims brought in from surrounding neighborhoods. "The prostitutes come in perpetually—poor creatures staggering off their beat! . . . One poor girl, loathsomely filthy, came in, and was dead in four hours," a friend recalled her saying. Nightingale worked day and night, removing patients' dirty clothes and placing cloths soaked in turpentine on their abdomens. These "turpentine stupes" were believed to ease internal upset.

A COURT FOR KING CHOLERA.

Miasma rises from decaying trash in crowded slums, and cholera results, according to this 1852 cartoon.

Around this time, a physician named John Snow figured out a way to stop the spread of cholera. Snow had studied earlier cholera outbreaks in London and had traced them to the water supply. He observed that most of the people dying in the 1854 epidemic lived near the Broad Street water pump. Area residents went to this pump to get water for their daily needs. "Take the handle off the Broad Street Pump," Snow said, and the epidemic will subside. Sure enough, when city officials removed the handle, making the pump unusable, new cases of cholera dwindled. Later researchers would demonstrate that cholera spread in cities when human waste containing disease-causing bacteria leaked into water systems.

With the crisis waning, Florence went to Lea Hurst for a few weeks of rest. There she met the author Elizabeth Gaskell, who was staying with the Nightingales while finishing a novel. Gaskell had gained loyal readers by writing about social issues, especially the challenges faced by women and life among the poor. The book she was writing at Lea Hurst, *North and South*, dealt with harsh working conditions in the cotton mills of northern England.

Jotting down her impression of Florence, Gaskell noted that she was "tall; very slight & willowy in figure," with "thick, shortish rich brown hair." Florence had "grey eyes which are generally pensive and drooping, but when they choose can be the merriest eyes I ever saw; and perfect teeth, making her smile the sweetest I ever saw."

In Florence, Gaskell spotted a brilliant mind and a strong sense of purpose. Florence made her think of Saint Elizabeth of Hungary, who had built a hospital and nursed the sick in the thirteenth century. Florence "must be a creature of another race, so high and mighty and angelic, doing things by impulse or some divine inspiration," Gaskell decided. "She seems as completely led by God as Joan of Arc. I never heard of any one like her."

No one can live up to such a lofty image. As a friendship grew between Gaskell and the Nightingales' other daughter, Gaskell's opinion of Florence changed. It seemed to Gaskell that Parthenope's "sense of existence is lost in Florence's." When Florence hesitated to visit a village woman whose husband had died, Gaskell saw proof that what Parthenope claimed was true: Florence cared only about grandiose plans for

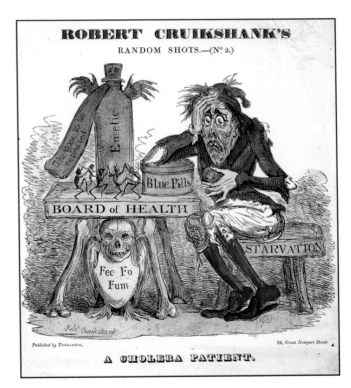

The treatments prescribed for cholera were as diverse and unscientific as the theories explaining its cause. It is no wonder that the patient in this cartoon is at a loss about what to do.

The writer Elizabeth Gaskell befriended the Nightingale family in 1854. Today Gaskell is best remembered as a biographer of novelist Charlotte Brontë.

hospitals, not about individual patients needing care. Neither Parthenope nor Elizabeth Gaskell had ever seen Florence hold a dying prostitute in her arms or tenderly nurse a governess recovering from cancer surgery, however.

Florence left for London in October with a new problem on her mind: the shameful care being given to British soldiers in wartime military hospitals. Britain was fighting a war on the Crimean Peninsula, where the balance of power was shifting. For hundreds of years, the city of Constantinople (now called Istanbul) had been the seat of the Ottoman Empire. This powerful Turkish state had long dominated the eastern Mediterranean Sea and the lands surrounding it, including Crimea. Now the empire was declining, and Russia, which had built up a strong military, was pushing for power in the region. On November 30, 1853, the Russian naval force had destroyed a fleet of Turkish ships at the port of Sinop and killed three thousand Turkish soldiers.

Britain and France declared war on Russia on March 28, 1854, because each had interests in the area to protect. Britain needed to guard its trade routes to its empire in the East, especially India. France wanted to prevent Russia from taking away its authority over Christians living in the Holy Land, a responsibility that the Ottoman Empire had granted to Napoleon III.

The Crimean War was different from earlier military conflicts. A recent innovation, the electric telegraph, was changing the way newspapers reported on fighting far from home. For the first time, journalists in the field could send news stories to their offices in a few hours rather than two weeks, the length of time it took to file a story by mail. People on the home front opened their morning papers to find vivid eyewitness accounts of battles fought just a day or two before.

Journalists exposed the horrifying conditions in army camps. The fifty thousand people who bought the *London Times* each day read with alarm about bad food that was being issued to their fighting men: "The beef being very like coarse mahogany. . . . The only attempt at butter is rancid lard packed in strong-smelling camel's-hair bags." The soldiers lacked waterproof gear and had too few blankets, and they often slept in torn tents that filled with water. Readers learned that "the wretched beggar who wanders about the streets of London in the rain, leads the life of a prince compared with the British soldiers who are fighting out here for their country."

On October 12, 1854, the *London Times* printed a shocking report on the care of sick and wounded soldiers. "Not only are there not sufficient surgeons," wrote one war correspondent, "not only are there no [wound] dressers and nurses . . . but what will be said when it is known that there is not even linen to make bandages for the wounded?" This shameful care began on the ships that carried the wounded from battle sites to the army hospital, the reporter revealed: "Not only are the men kept, in some cases, for a week without the hand of a medical man coming near their wounds—not only are they left to expire in agony, unheeded and shaken off, though catching desperately at the surgeon whenever he makes his rounds through the fetid ship, but now, when they are placed in the spacious building . . . men must die through the medical staff of the British army having forgotten that old rags are necessary for the dressing of wounds." Untrained male orderlies were nursing the men but doing it badly. Meanwhile, French soldiers in their military hospitals were being tended by Sisters of Charity. On October 14, the *London Times* published a letter from an irate reader who asked, "Why have we no Sisters of Charity?"

Florence Nightingale was asking a similar question. In fact, she was already making plans without her parents' knowledge. She proposed to Lord Palmerston, an old family friend who was the government's home secretary, that she go to the war zone. She would take along another nurse, whose salary she would pay. As Palmerston sent her offer up the chain of command, Nightingale wrote about it to the Herberts. Sidney Herbert was again serving as secretary of war, and Nightingale wanted his advice on the best way to carry out her plan.

French Sisters of Charity nurse soldiers on the battlefield.

Before he had a chance to see her letter, Herbert sent her one of his own. He believed that a group of female nurses would be of great benefit at the Barrack Hospital at Scutari (now the Üsküdar district of Istanbul). "I receive numbers of offers from ladies to go out," Herbert wrote, "but they are ladies who have no conception of what an Hospital is, nor of the nature of its duties, & they would, when the time came, either recoil from the work, or be entirely useless." He went on to say, "There is but one person in England that I know of, who would be capable of organizing & superintending such a scheme." He asked that one person, Florence Nightingale, if she would "undertake to direct it." He warned, "The difficulty of finding women equal to a task after all full of horror, & requiring besides knowledge & goodwill, great energy, & great courage will be great. The task of ruling them & introducing system among them, great; & not least, will be the difficulty of making the whole work smoothly with the medical & military authorities out there."

Herbert worried that Florence's parents might deny her permission to go. But they could hardly refuse an urgent request from the government, especially after the Bracebridges offered to accompany Florence to Scutari as chaperones and helpers. Even Parthe approved of her sister's mission. It seemed to her that all of Florence's experience had prepared her for this moment. "None of her previous life has been wasted," Parthe commented.

Sidney Herbert made Nightingale's appointment official. He drew up paperwork naming her "Superintendent of the female nursing establishment in the English General Military Hospitals in Turkey." She was to have complete authority over the forty nurses she supervised, including the power to dismiss them as she saw fit. Employing female nurses in British military hospitals had never been tried. No one knew how it was going to work.

Herbert introduced his plan to the public in the press. "Miss Nightingale," he wrote, had "greater practical experience of hospital administration and treatment than any other lady in this country." Lest they think Nightingale was doing something unnatural, he assured readers that she understood her place as a woman. "She will act in the strictest subordination to the chief medical officer of the hospital," he stated. He added, "No additional nurses will be sent out to her until she shall have written home from Scutari, and reported how far her labours have been successful, and what number and description of persons, if any, she requires in addition."

With just days to find forty nurses and organize her expedition, Nightingale set up headquarters in the Herberts' London home. Liz Herbert and Parthenope helped her sort through the many letters that arrived from all over England. Household servants and widows were among the women who offered to join the group. Some were prompted by patriotism, others by desire for adventure or for the twelve to fourteen shillings a week that Scutari nurses were to be paid. Nightingale found thirty-eight women to hire: fourteen Anglican nursing sisters, ten Roman Catholic nuns, and fourteen others, among them her housekeeper from Upper Harley Street, Mary Clarke. Sidney Herbert had obtained government approval for the Catholics to be included. They were important to the mission, he believed, because Irish soldiers made up a third of the British fighting force in the Crimea, and most of those ten thousand Irishmen were Catholic.

As Florence was preparing for her journey, she received a letter of support from her mother. "God speed you on your errand of mercy, my own dearest child," Fanny Nightingale wrote. A loving parent, Mrs. Nightingale urged her daughter to take care. "I do not ask you to spare yourself for your own sake," she said in closing, "but for the sake of the cause."

The British humor magazine *Punch* depicted Nightingale as a bird and one of her nurses as a ministering angel.

Another letter took Florence by surprise. It came from Richard Monckton Milnes. "I hear you are going to the East. I am happy it is so, for the good you will do there, and the hope that you may find some satisfaction in it yourself," he wrote. He had been distant at their last meeting, and now he revealed that her failure to accept his proposal still caused him grief. "You can undertake [the mission to Scutari], when you could not undertake with me," he continued. "God bless you, dear Friend, wherever you go." Florence kept this letter for the rest of her life.

A third message reached Florence on the day before she was to leave England. It came from Lea Hurst, and it brought the sad news that Athena had died. Florence delayed her departure for two days while a servant carried the wee body to London. Flo cried as it was placed in her hands. "Poor little beastie," she whispered, stroking its feathers. "It was odd how much I loved you."

CHAPTER 7

The Horrors

IT was like a huge slaughter-house." This was the only way Sister St. George could describe the Barrack Hospital at Scutari. Upon entering, she and the other nurses saw "wounded men lying with mangled limbs on the open pavements. . . . Most of them, even apart from wounds, were half-dead with cold and exposure. Some had been six weeks in the trenches, with their flesh frozen to their clothes." Half a century later, this Catholic nun could still exclaim, "Such a scene! Never shall I forget the horrors of that hospital at Scutari!"

The Reverend Sydney Osborne, there to minister to the sick and wounded, felt that he had walked into a "vast field of suffering, and misery." In every ward and hallway he saw men writhing, moaning, and dying. An entire corridor had been set aside for storing the dead. "I had passed weeks in the West of Ireland when famine was slaying its hundreds daily," he said. "I had seen a good deal of cholera on a large scale." Yet nothing in his experience had prepared Osborne for Scutari. Men with dysentery or open wounds lay on sheets that had not been changed for months. They wore shirts that were in "a condition disgusting to see." It was no wonder, Osborne said, that the smell in the wards was at times "so offensive as to be scarcely endurable even to the oldest Medical Officers." He was "inexpressibly shocked."

Scutari sat on the eastern, or Asian, side of the Bosporus Strait. It was known for its Turkish burial grounds, which had been called "the largest, the most beautiful, and the most justly celebrated" in the Ottoman Empire. The graves included the canopied resting place of a sultan's horse. Not far away, in the open markets and poor neighborhoods, stray dogs scavenged in the dirty streets. Across the water, on the European side of the Bosporus, the white buildings and minarets of Constantinople gleamed in the sunlight.

The Barrack Hospital had been built in 1800 to quarter Turkish soldiers. During the Crimean War, Turkey offered it to the British, who turned it into a treatment center. It was so enormous that "the world wondered if the whole British army were

The Barrack Hospital, viewed from a Turkish cemetery, was a mammoth structure.

An artist imagined the scene Nightingale encountered at Scutari.

going into hospital," remarked an American missionary in Constantinople. Each of its four sides measured roughly six hundred feet—more than a tenth of a mile; Charles Bracebridge counted five hundred paces as he walked the length of its longest corridor. The structure was three stories high with a tower at each corner, and it was built around a courtyard. This open space had been a military parade ground for the Turks, but the British used it as a muddy garbage dump. The Barrack Hospital had space for twelve hundred patients, but it housed two thousand. Wards large enough for thirty men held seventy-two. Nightingale discovered two hundred women living in the hospital's dark, smelly cellars. Some were prostitutes, others were soldiers' wives, and several had children. Many of the women and children were sick.

Nightingale assigned ten nurses to the smaller General Hospital, half a mile away, which was dealing with a horrendous diarrhea outbreak. Sick officers filled the General Hospital's wards, and ailing enlisted men crowded the halls. All the men shared twenty chamber pots and a few reeking latrines.

The nurses set up living quarters in the Barrack Hospital's northwest tower, which was as filthy and rundown as the rest of the place. Rats, fleas, bedbugs, and lice infested the rooms. Storms caused havoc in the dilapidated tower. "Occasionally the roof is torn off our quarters," Nightingale wrote to a doctor in England, "or the windows blown in—and we are flooded and under water for the night."

Nightingale, the Bracebridges, and the thirty-eight nurses occupied seven rooms on three levels, the amount of space typically allotted to three junior medical officers and their servants. Nightingale and her team set aside a large room for storage and turned a smaller one into a kitchen. On its portable stoves they cooked broth and other easy-to-digest foods for the sickest men. There were no chairs or tables; the nursing party had to sit and eat on the floor. Nightingale slept on a cot behind a curtain in the tower room that served as her office. It was "a wee room," she said, full of "bad smells."

Each woman had a copper basin to hold water for washing and drinking, but the water that dripped out of the hospital fountains was so cloudy and dingy that most drank beer or wine instead. Nightingale put up with occasional drunkenness among the nurses because she had no choice. But over the months, some women grew dependent on alcohol and had to be sent home.

Although the younger doctors welcomed the nurses' help, most of the senior medical officers resented the women's presence. They called Nightingale "the Bird" behind her back, gave her sour looks, and ordered her and her staff to stay out of their hospital wards. These men shared the attitude of Dr. John Hall, the chief medical officer in the East. He opposed any kind of change, even if it might have benefits. While other doctors had started using chloroform to put patients to sleep during surgery, Hall preferred to keep them awake and alert, "to hear a man bawl lustily." He swore that "the smart of a knife" was "a powerful stimulant." Hall had made up his mind about the women well before they arrived. Nightingale was sure to be a rich, meddling busybody looking for adventure. The others were going to be no better than the hospital nurses he recalled from earlier years in England: ignorant and of questionable character.

How infuriating! But Nightingale's orders were to serve as the doctors saw fit. She was powerless to act, no matter how much her staff complained. "We tried to console ourselves by making flannel shirts and bandages," said Sarah Anne Terrot, a Protestant nursing sister. Others scrubbed walls and floors. The nurses were bored, though, and some found fault with everything, including the uniforms they had been

Dr. John Hall was a career army medical officer who had served throughout the British Empire, from Jamaica to South Africa to India. He looked upon Nightingale as a threat to his authority.

given to wear. One grumpy woman complained that her cap did nothing to flatter her face. She told Nightingale, "If I'd known, Ma'am, about the caps, great as was my desire to come out to nurse at Scutari, I wouldn't have come." The Catholic nuns and Protestant nursing sisters wore the habits and uniforms of their orders, but the rest were issued black woolen dresses, white linen aprons, and the unpopular caps. The dresses were all the same size, so some women were stuck wearing ill-fitting clothes.

Nightingale dressed no better. "She has one flannel petticoat left," Selina Bracebridge reported to Parthenope, "one bonnet with a hole in it — her black gowns (& she wears no others) are very grubby."

It was a frustrating time for Nightingale and her nurses, but very soon the doctors turned to them for help. They had no choice: two recent battles had left thousands of casualties, and many men were being transported to the Barrack Hospital; "400 wounded arriving *at this moment* for us to nurse," Nightingale wrote hastily to her family. Hundreds more were on the way.

On October 25, 1854, the British and their allies fought the Russians in the Battle of Balaclava. This battle is remembered for the disastrous charge of a British cavalry force known as the Light Brigade. Someone misunderstood an order, and the result was a costly, tragic mistake. The horsemen of the Light Brigade rode into a valley and discovered too late that they were surrounded by Russian guns. The *London Times* reporter on the scene described the belching forth "from thirty iron-mouths, a flood of smoke and flame, through which hissed the deadly balls." A horde of enemy soldiers rushed down upon the British and sliced at them with swords. Of the more than six hundred British cavalrymen who made the ill-fated charge, one hundred and fifty-six were killed. "The plain was strewed with their bodies, and with the carcases of their horses," the newsman wrote. Another one hundred and twenty-two men were wounded but survived.

The Russians were the victors at Balaclava, but Britain won the bloody Battle of Inkerman, eleven days later. Early on the foggy morning of November 5, a British

Britain's Light Brigade rides into enemy fire. The charge of the Light Brigade is remembered as a tragic military blunder.

unit was starting fires to cook breakfast when the Russians advanced on them. All at once the entire camp "seemed encircled by fire, as flash after flash lit up the foggy air in all directions," a newspaperman reported. "The uproar was perfectly deafening." Men threw themselves face-down on the ground as artillery shells flew overhead in all directions. Other British forces hurried to their aid and fought fiercely, often firing blindly in the thick mist, to drive the Russians back. The *London Times* called the battle "the boldest struggle ever witnessed since war cursed the earth." When it was over, the British counted 597 soldiers dead and 1,860 wounded.

With so many incoming casualties, the nurses had unending work to do. There were men who had been patched up on the field of battle. Blood had soaked into their bandages and dried, gluing the cloth to their wounds. The nurses had to soak these dirty old bandages off before the wounds could be cleaned and new wrappings could be applied. They sewed sacks and stuffed them with straw to make mattresses for men lying on the floor. In the tower kitchen, Mary Clarke cooked kettles of broth. The Reverend Sydney Osborne hurried from one wounded soldier to another, offering prayers and comfort and writing letters for patients to their loved ones at home. Osborne knew that for some men, these letters would be their last.

Even after the rush of new patients slowed, the nurses stayed busy. Nightingale and her staff battled disease as they believed best: by clearing away miasma. They mopped and swept; they opened windows that had been boarded up and let in fresher air. They could have done much more if only they had had supplies. "There was neither basin, towel nor soap in the wards," Nightingale reported, "nor any means of personal cleanliness for the wounded." A soldier was lucky to be bathed once in eighty days. Medical officers had so few sponges that they used the same ones over and over to wash wound after wound.

The *London Times* had started a fund so citizens could donate money to aid the sick and wounded soldiers. Nightingale drew on this fund to buy shirts for men who had not put on clean clothes since they were struck in battle weeks before. The *Times* sent its business manager, John Macdonald, to Scutari to make sure the donations were wisely spent. He and Charles Bracebridge ventured into the markets of Constantinople for Nightingale. She gave them a shopping list that included items as basic as saucepans, combs, sheets, and wooden spoons. Nightingale also used money from the fund to lease a building to use as a laundry so that all the patients could enjoy clean clothes and bedding. She found laundry workers among the women who had been living below the hospital. She also located a portable screen to be placed around a patient having an arm or leg cut off. "For when one poor fellow—who is to be amputated tomorrow—sees his comrade today die under the knife, it makes impression," she explained, "and diminishes his chance."

Nightingale saved at least one man from losing a limb and possibly his life. He was a soldier named Samuel Atkins whose arm had been badly wounded in the Battle of Inkerman. A surgeon at the Barrack Hospital wanted to remove it, but Nightingale thought this doctor was being too hasty. She told Atkins he showed no sign of infection and advised him to refuse the procedure. Much later, Atkins recalled Nightingale saying "that they could not take it off without my permission and that my arm would look better in my sleeve than the sleeve would look in my waistcoat pocket." For the rest of his life, Atkins remained grateful for Nightingale's good counsel.

Charles Bracebridge saw the doctors' opinion of Florence Nightingale change. "Flo has in this week not only gained the love but the confidence of all. The doctors do her will," he observed. He remarked on "the deathbeds—poor Flo sees five or six expire every day, and feels each one as if she had never seen one before."

Nightingale and her nurses accomplished much good, but problems lingered. For example, shortages remained a constant headache. A requisition for supplies had to go first to the chief medical officer in England. It next had to pass from one bureaucrat's desk to another before the goods could be ordered. The staff in Scutari then had to wait for the needed items to be manufactured and shipped to the hospitals. Even

In this painting by the English artist Jerry Barrett, Florence Nightingale receives wounded soldiers at Scutari. She wears a brown dress and white cap and stands between Charles and Selina Bracebridge. Barrett traveled to Scutari, where he sketched this scene. He completed the painting after he returned to England.

then, delivery was not ensured. Some cargoes were pilfered along the way or sent to the wrong port. A ship laden with hospital supplies and coats and boots for the soldiers in the field sank during a storm. Also, the purveyor of supplies—the army officer in charge of ordering goods—cared more about cutting costs than stocking items the hospitals needed.

The people of Britain responded to reports of shortages by sending linen for bandages, handmade slippers for the soldiers, and cookies and jam from their kitchens. Others sent money so Nightingale could buy the things she needed most. A supply of scarves came from Queen Victoria. The queen wanted Nightingale to distribute her gift to the patients and nurses.

"I am really cook, house-keeper, scavenger . . . washerwoman, general dealer, store-keeper," Nightingale wrote about herself. At times she spent twenty hours on her feet, doing all she could "for these miserable Hospitals as long as I have power to do so."

Providing decent food was another difficulty. In December 1854, one of the nurses wrote home, "We have not seen a drop of milk, and the bread is extremely sour." She added, "The meat is more like moist leather than food." When the *London Illustrated News* printed this letter, it caught the attention of Alexis Soyer, the city's most famous chef. The French-born Soyer had cooked in London's finest restaurants and clubs. But he had also opened soup kitchens in Dublin to feed starving people during the Irish famine of the 1840s. Once back in London, he had done the same thing for that city's poor. He was sure he could improve the meals being served in the army hospitals. With his cheerful nature and carefree charm, Soyer easily persuaded the War Office to send him and his assistants to Scutari.

Upon arriving, Soyer sought out Florence Nightingale. He met a woman "rather high of stature, fair in complexion, and slim in person," he noted. "Her eyes, of a bluish tint, speak volumes, and are always sparking with intelligence." He remarked on her dress, which was "generally of a greyish or black tint; she wears a simple white cap, and often a rough apron." The chef who introduced himself to Nightingale was tall and stocky with short gray hair and a closely trimmed mustache. His bright wardrobe matched his showy personality. (Soyer was known to wear yellow gloves and lavender-trimmed trousers.) But he was all business when he went to work.

Chef Alexis Soyer was a flamboyant figure who used his skills and celebrity to accomplish good. Thanks to his selfless efforts, the soldiers in British army hospitals enjoyed healthy, palatable food.

When he saw the Barrack Hospital and the number of patients needing to be fed, his "mind was quite overpowered," Soyer admitted. He began by inspecting the hospital kitchens. He noticed the filthy cauldrons used to boil the patients' meat and tea and the poor-quality charcoal that fueled the stove. He oversaw a thorough scouring and bought a new stove and better charcoal. Then he went to work on the food. He solved the problem of badly cooked meat by cutting up raw meat and putting it into a soup along with barley, vegetables, and potatoes. The soldiers welcomed the warm, flavorful result made from ingredients on hand. Soyer also devised recipes for easily digested invalid meals. Just as important, he taught the hospital's kitchen staff how to cook and season food.

Newspaper reports of lost battles, military mistakes, and poor treatment of soldiers made many people want to help. But they also made the British public angry about the way their government was managing the war. By the time Soyer arrived at Scutari, Britain had voted the ruling party out of office and elected a new government. Eager to make changes, the new prime minister, Lord Palmerston, formed a sanitary commission and dispatched it to Scutari. Its mission was to "exert all that science can do to save life, where thousands are dying, not of their wounds, but of dysentery and diarrhea."

The commission began its task in early March 1855. In the Barrack Hospital its members saw "marks of much having been done to improve it," but deplorable conditions remained. The sewers below the hospital were clogged. "The wind blew sewer air up the pipes of numerous open privies into the corridors and wards in which the sick lay," the commission reported. A dead horse was lodged in the main water pipe; privies were leaking into nearby water tanks. These health hazards were too large for the nurses to tackle, but the commissioners had authority to correct them. They ordered walls whitewashed and rotting floors replaced. They had vents cut in the roof, allowing air to circulate. The doctor who headed the sanitary commission, John Sutherland, became Nightingale's loyal friend. He was a Scotsman with years of experience working in public health. He was a learned man who liked a good joke, but he had a strong will when there was work to be done.

Throughout the winter and into the spring of 1855, Nightingale and her nurses kept the convalescing soldiers clean and dressed in freshly laundered shirts. They boiled bed linens to kill lice. Nurses and orderlies scrubbed every possible surface. Alexis Soyer worked his wonders in the kitchen. The sanitary commission tackled big jobs. And the death rate at the Scutari hospitals fell. In February, half the men who were admitted died. In March, only a fifth were dying. The number of deaths fell

Dr. John Sutherland was photographed in a makeshift studio in the war zone. Sutherland, who went to Scutari with the sanitary commission, became Nightingale's friend. After the war, he worked with her on improving health in the peacetime army.

further in the months ahead. Nightingale stated with pride, "*We* pulled this Hospital through for 4 months & without us, it would have come to a stand-still."

If Nightingale had one shortcoming, it was her management style. She expected the nurses to obey her without question. They were there to work, and it seemed to her that giving them explanations wasted time. Some unhappy nurses complained about Miss Nightingale's curtness. One day, a senior nurse among the Anglican sisters, a Miss Jones, advised Nightingale to encourage the women and treat them kindly. Nightingale replied that she had no time for such trifles and hurried off to her next task. But Jones's words sank in, and Nightingale tried harder to be a considerate leader. She worked to create the representative system that her father had recommended.

Still, she never relaxed her strict rules. She told the nurses that if called to a patient's bedside, they were to do the doctor's bidding, quietly and professionally. It was all right to speak to the patient in calming tones but not to tire him in conversation. There was to be no flirting or discussion of religious beliefs. The nurses were to remember at all times that they were being observed. The unprofessional conduct of one reflected badly on them all.

Nightingale always had time for the hospitalized men. She was on hand when they had surgery and often tended to them in the wards. "Her nerve is wonderful," said the Reverend Sydney Osborne. "I have known her spend hours over men dying of cholera or fever. The more awful to every sense any particular case, especially if it was that of a dying man, her slight form would be seen bending over him, administering to his ease in every way in her power, and seldom quitting his side till death released him."

CHAPTER 8

An Angel with a Lamp

JOHN Macdonald, who had overseen the *London Times*'s Crimea fund, went home to England and wrote about Florence Nightingale for his newspaper. "She is a 'ministering angel,'" he told the paper's readers. "As her slender form glides along each corridor, every poor fellow's face softens with gratitude at the sight of her." Late at night, when the doctors were asleep and the sick men lay in darkness, "she may be observed alone," Macdonald noted, "with a little lamp in her hand making her solitary rounds." Another newspaper printed a sketch of Nightingale standing at the foot of a soldier's bed. An oil lamp glows in her hand, giving off the only light in the crowded ward.

At a time when the papers were full of distressing accounts of war, people clung to any good news. All of Britain was curious about the Lady with the Lamp. She was doing something so unusual that the public wanted to know if she was indeed a proper lady. Did she draw strength from moral virtue? Was she governed by religious faith?

Some who had met Nightingale wrote articles and books assuring readers that she was principled and devout. "In conversation no member of the fair sex can be more amiable and gentle than Miss Nightingale," wrote chef Alexis Soyer. The Reverend Sydney Osborne attested that he found her a Christian in "her every word and action." He added, "Her work ought to answer for her faith."

"Her happiest place is at home," claimed one less-than-truthful writer, "in simplest obedience to her admiring parents." He concluded his report honestly, stating, "There is not one of England's proudest and purest daughters who at this moment stands on so high a pinnacle as Florence Nightingale."

Nightingale's relatives were getting attention too. People gathered around them

The British public saw images of Florence Nightingale carrying an oil lamp like the ones often pictured in illustrations for *The Arabian Nights*, a collection of stories from the Middle East and Asia.

at parties, eager to learn about the illustrious nurse. The travel writer Elisabeth C. H. Gray praised Fanny Nightingale for being "the mother of so heroic a woman." Even more thrilling for Fanny, Queen Victoria invited the Nightingales to watch from Buckingham Palace's front courtyard as soldiers freshly home from the war paraded past.

Fanny stood proudly, knowing the queen and her children were on the balcony above. (In 1840 Victoria had married one of her cousins, Prince Albert of Saxe-Coburg. By this time in 1855 Victoria and Albert had produced eight of the nine children they were to have.) Fanny, from her spot, observed the rows of

In reality, Nightingale usually carried a Turkish lantern that was designed to hold a candle.

"fine fellows, care worn & weary, in thin old Crimean clothes" marching just a few feet away. She thought of Florence and said, "It was most touching to be in such close contact with some of those for whom she has been toiling."

Florence's father spent the day at home. William Nightingale did "not like celebrity," Fanny explained to a friend. The many curious strangers who came knocking at his door drew Mr. Nightingale away from his reading. One day, while enjoying a solitary walk on the grounds of Lea Hurst, he bumped into a snooping army officer. The man praised Florence and her work; he predicted that when she was again in London, she would be carried through the streets. "What next?" William Nightingale complained to his wife. "Will she call the dead to life?"

And then there was Parthenope. For years Parthe had struggled painfully in her younger sister's shadow. When Flo took charge of the Establishment for Gentlewomen, Parthe had tried to change and offer support. Now, at last, Parthe had work of her own to do. She clipped articles mentioning Flo from newspapers and magazines and glued them into scrapbooks. She answered the many letters that arrived from Flo's admirers. Some people sent gifts; others wrote songs or poems in Flo's honor. Letters came from soldiers who had been under Nightingale's care. In the hospital "she's here, there, and everywhere," stated one. "You never lose sight of her." Parthe was almost bragging when she informed a cousin, "The immense amount of writing which I have to do is incredible, in my sister's cause."

No one knew better than Florence Nightingale herself how different the popular image of her was from the real woman performing exhausting, dirty work. "Good public! It knew nothing of what I was really doing in the Crimea," she later said.

Florence Nightingale was famous, but she was not the only nursing pioneer to aid wounded soldiers during the Crimean War. Jamaican-born Mary Seacole went to the war zone on her own. A descendant of enslaved Africans, Seacole had learned medical practices and herbal treatments as a nurse in Jamaica and Panama. She had applied in London to be one of Nightingale's nurses, but Liz Herbert had turned her down, possibly because of her race.

Seacole reached Scutari and presented herself at the Barrack Hospital. There she "came upon the long wards of sufferers, lying there so quiet and still," she recalled. "Some of the convalescent formed themselves into little groups around one who read a newspaper; others had books in their hands, or by their side, where they had fallen when slumber overtook the readers, while hospital orderlies moved to and fro, and

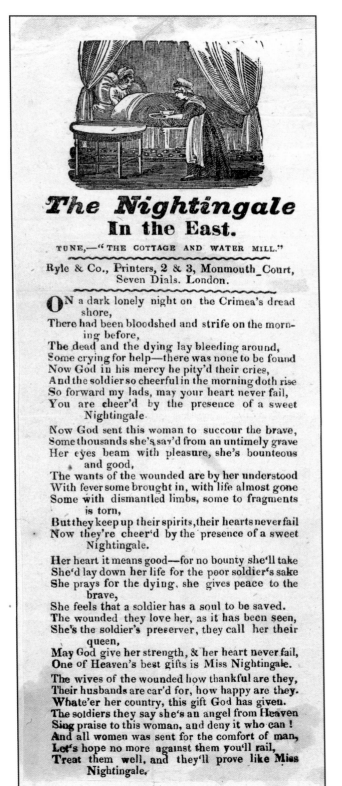

The Nightingale In the East.

TUNE,—"THE COTTAGE AND WATER MILL."

Ryle & Co., Printers, 2 & 3, Monmouth Court,
Seven Dials. London.

ON a dark lonely night on the Crimea's dread
    shore,
There had been bloodshed and strife on the morn-
    ing before,
The dead and the dying lay bleeding around,
Some crying for help—there was none to be found
Now God in his mercy he pity'd their cries,
And the soldier so cheerful in the morning doth rise
So forward my lads, may your heart never fail,
You are cheer'd by the presence of a sweet
    Nightingale.

Now God sent this woman to succour the brave,
Some thousands she's sav'd from an untimely grave
Her eyes beam with pleasure, she's bounteous
    and good,
The wants of the wounded are by her understood
With fever some brought in, with life almost gone
Some with dismantled limbs, some to fragments
    is torn,
But they keep up their spirits, their hearts never fail
Now they're cheer'd by the presence of a sweet
    Nightingale.

Her heart it means good—for no bounty she'll take
She'd lay down her life for the poor soldier's sake
She prays for the dying, she gives peace to the
    brave,
She feels that a soldier has a soul to be saved.
The wounded they love her, as it has been seen,
She's the soldier's preserver, they call her their
    queen,
May God give her strength, & her heart never fail,
One of Heaven's best gifts is Miss Nightingale.

The wives of the wounded how thankful are they,
Their husbands are car'd for, how happy are they.
Whate'er her country, this gift God has given.
The soldiers they say she's an angel from Heaven
Sing praise to this woman, and deny it who can !
And all women was sent for the comfort of man,
Let's hope no more against them you'll rail,
Treat them well, and they'll prove like Miss
    Nightingale.

now and then the female nurses, in their quiet uniform, passed noiselessly on some mission of kindness."

Selina Bracebridge, flustered at the sight of a black nurse, told Seacole there were no vacancies on the hospital staff. When Seacole explained that she was on her way to Balaclava, Mrs. Bracebridge asked her to stay in the nurses' kitchen and went to fetch Nightingale. While Seacole waited, she watched nurses pass in and out of the room. "Many of them had that strange expression of the eyes which those who have gazed long on scenes of woe and horror seldom lose," she said. A half hour later she met Florence Nightingale. She saw "a slight figure, in the nurses' dress; with a pale, gentle, and withal firm face, resting lightly in the palm of one white hand, while the other supports the elbow." Nightingale's face bore "a keen inquiring expression." If she showed any sign of

"The Nightingale in the East": An admirer wrote these lyrics celebrating Florence Nightingale. They were to be sung to the tune of a traditional ballad.

impatience, it was "a slight, perhaps unwitting motion of the firmly planted right foot."

Nightingale let Seacole spend a night in the washerwomen's quarters before continuing on to Balaclava. There, near that famed battle site, Seacole used packing crates and other discarded materials to build a hotel for convalescing officers. She served meals and dispensed herbal remedies; at times she carried bandages and medicines onto the battlefield to treat wounded men. The soldiers called her Aunty or Mother and watched for her bright yellow dress.

Mary Seacole, who was born in Jamaica, provided aid and comfort to men wounded in battle.

More troubling to Nightingale was the appearance of Mary Stanley, whom she had met in Italy in 1848. Seeking novelty and a measure of fame for herself, Stanley had persuaded Sidney Herbert to send her to Scutari. She came with fifteen Irish Catholic Sisters of Mercy, some twenty lay nurses, and nine lady volunteers. When Nightingale learned in December 1854 that the Stanley party was on its way, she flew into a temper. Herbert had assured her that new nurses were to be sent to Scutari only if Nightingale requested them. How could she supervise this many women? Where was she to house them? What would they eat and drink? She knew nothing of their qualifications—if they lacked training, they might undo all the good she had accomplished.

Feeling betrayed, Nightingale lashed out at Herbert in an angry letter. "You have sacrificed the cause so near my heart," she wrote. "You have sacrificed me, a matter of small importance now." She knew how to solve the problem of Mary Stanley, however.

Keeping her emotions under control, she asked Stanley to come see her. Then, in front of Charles Bracebridge and one of the hospital's physicians, Nightingale announced that she was resigning. From that moment forward, Mary Stanley would oversee nursing in the Scutari hospitals. As Nightingale expected, Stanley burst into tears. The job was too big for someone like Stanley, who had never managed anything. She then had to humble herself by asking Nightingale for a loan. It seemed she had spent all her money while traveling to Turkey.

Nightingale's resignation was a bluff. With her authority affirmed, she found places for most of Mary Stanley's nurses. A few had sound nursing experience and remained at the Barrack Hospital. Stanley and some others went to a new hospital five miles away, at Koulali. A third group, which included the Irish nuns, was sent to an army hospital on the Crimean Peninsula, across the Black Sea. Three months later Mary Stanley returned to England, having had enough of wartime nursing. From then on, new nurses arrived only when Nightingale herself requested them.

When Nightingale first offered her services to the government, she was given control of the female nurses in Turkey. Since then, women had moved into military hospitals in other parts of the region, such as the Crimean Peninsula, which were beyond the limits of her authority. Nightingale was trying to maintain her high standards, but she was feeling frustrated. She had little say about which nurses worked in the more distant hospitals and how they conducted themselves. She wanted to go to the Crimean Peninsula to visit hospitals there.

The Bracebridges urged Nightingale not to make the three-hundred-mile trip. She was worn out, and so were they. In fact, they wished she would leave the military hospitals and go home to England; she certainly had done enough. Nightingale would not hear of it, though. She journeyed to Crimea in May 1855 with Charles Bracebridge

dutifully by her side. Traveling with them were four nurses, chef Alexis Soyer and his servant, and a twelve-year-old drummer boy named Thomas who called himself Miss Nightingale's man. They sailed on a ship carrying soldiers who had regained enough of their health to go back to the fight.

After reaching the place where so many had battled and died, Nightingale and her party visited an army camp, where the men numbered in the thousands. The soldiers gave the celebrated nurse three cheers, and she heard them with a grateful heart. "I took it as a full reward of all I have gone through," she confided to her family at home. "I promised my God that I would not die of disgust or disappointment, if he would let me go through this."

She and the others rode horses to a high point from which they looked down on Sebastopol. Below they saw thousands more soldiers amassing for upcoming battles. It was spring, and around the horses' hooves bloomed tiny red roses and fragrant yellow trumpets of jasmine. "This is the most flowery place you can imagine," Florence wrote to Parthenope. The blossoms were small reminders of beauty and hope in a wartime landscape.

A sergeant escorting Nightingale picked her a nosegay. She knew this man and recalled how she had saved his life one night. He had been lying in the hospital "with a bullet in his eye & a fractured skull," and no doctor had come by to treat him. She had "pulled a stray Surgeon out of bed" and commanded him to take the bullet out.

Nightingale toured the General Hospital at Balaclava, which had been a village school before the war. She went to the newer Castle Hospital, which was really just a collection of huts. She saw that the soldiers all had beds and blankets, but

In this painting by the artist Jerry Barrett, Nightingale and the Bracebridges seek shade beneath an overhanging roof while walking in a Turkish street. By spring 1855, the Bracebridges wanted Nightingale to give up her war work and go home.

Nightingale cares for a recovering soldier while sailing to the Crimean Peninsula.

they needed much more. Clothes sent to the laundry came back no cleaner, and the General Hospital's privies gave off a suffocating odor. Nightingale could do nothing, though, because Dr. John Hall, the closed-minded physician in charge, still opposed her. He declared that all her requests for the two hospitals had to be submitted to him, and Nightingale knew he would never approve them. At least she and Alexis Soyer improved the food served to the men.

In the Crimean hospitals, Nightingale sat with the feverish men. Soyer warned her to use caution lest she become sick as well, but Nightingale scoffed at his worries. She was used to being near illness, she said, and had no fear of infection. But Florence Nightingale did get sick. On May 13, the day after her thirty-fifth birthday, she woke with a soaring fever. Feeling so heavy with fatigue that she could barely walk, she consulted Dr. Arthur Anderson, who oversaw the General Hospital at Balaclava. Anderson took one look at Nightingale and diagnosed an illness he had seen often since coming to war. The English called it Crimean fever, and Nightingale had "as bad an attack of fever as I have seen," Anderson said.

The modern term for this disease is brucellosis. It is a bacterial illness that people contract by consuming the milk or meat of infected animals, usually goats. Today doctors treat brucellosis with antibiotics, but in the 1850s no one knew its cause or its cure. Once the bacteria entered a person's system, they found their way into the body's cells, where they remained. For the rest of the person's life, pain, fever, and exhaustion came and went. Florence Nightingale would never be entirely well again.

At first she was too ill even to feed herself. Her doctors and friends urged her to go home, but she insisted on staying where she was needed. So the Bracebridges readied a small house in Scutari where she could convalesce, and she spent part of the

From a high ridge, Florence Nightingale and Charles Bracebridge look down on the graves of British soldiers who died in the Battle of Inkerman.

Nightingale braved rugged terrain to visit a hospital that was little more than a group of huts.

summer at the seaside, in the home of the British ambassador. Her hair was cut short to keep her cool during times of fever. She looked suddenly older and distressingly thin.

To cheer her, Parthenope sent a small book she had made, *The Life and Death of Athena, an Owlet from the Parthenon.* In words and pictures, Parthe told the story of the orphaned bird that had brightened the Nightingales' lives with her love and mischief. "Her qualities of soul heart and intellect, were indeed first rate," Parthe stated about Athena. Florence wrote in thanks, "I cannot tell you how the record of Athena's little life & death affected us all. It is worth while to have died to be so remembered."

Gradually Nightingale gained enough strength to stand for a brief time. By midsummer, however, the Bracebridges had made up their minds. Even if Florence was determined to stay, they were returning to England. Selina had had enough; the months of hard work were harming her own health. So that Florence would not be left on her own, her beloved aunt Mai Smith took the Bracebridges' place at her side.

Smith was shocked to see the striking change in her niece that illness had brought about. Still, she did her best to reassure the Nightingales in her letters to England, informing them that Flo "looks pretty well," if "altered." Smith wrote, "It is the firmness of her voice that comforts me," and she crossed her fingers that the words sounded hopeful.

The hospitals at Scutari were running smoothly, but Nightingale had much more yet to do. She set up a money-order office so the men could send part of their pay home to their families. She wanted to create reading rooms and offer classes for the convalescing soldiers, who needed diversions. Many were lessening their boredom with alcohol. "Give them books and games and amusements, and they will leave off drinking," Nightingale asserted. In England, Parthe collected donations of books and magazines, pens and paper, games, sheet music for sing-alongs, and scripts for staging plays.

Florence also had reams of writing to do. She recorded hospital statistics, drafted reports, and answered worried inquiries from patients' loved ones. After doing all that, she sent condolence letters to the families of hospitalized soldiers who had died.

Autumn arrived, and the war was nearing its end. The Russians were retreating, and the number of wounded soldiers was dropping. The hospital at Koulali no longer needed the Catholic nuns who had come with Mary Stanley. Nightingale could have used them at Scutari, but the nun who led them,

Parthenope Nightingale's charming drawings of Athena brightened the spirits of her ailing sister.

Mother Mary Francis Bridgeman, refused to take orders from her. Bridgeman went behind Nightingale's back and got Dr. Hall's approval to bring the sisters across the water to the General Hospital at Balaclava.

Nightingale believed all the Crimean War nurses should be her responsibility, including "Mother Brickbat." But the only thing Nightingale could do in this situation was escort Bridgeman and the other Sisters of Charity as they sailed from Turkey to Balaclava. Nightingale thought it was important to make the trip, although this display of control was only for show. She left Aunt Mai to run the Barrack Hospital.

Nothing went right for Nightingale at Balaclava. She was seasick during the voyage, Bridgeman's nuns were hostile to her, and she was in constant pain from Crimean fever. Mother Bridgeman and Dr. Hall quickly became cozy friends, which made it harder than ever for Nightingale to get requisitions approved. She returned to Scutari feeling discouraged.

She still felt low when she attended the British ambassador's Christmas party. Another guest, a lady, was surprised at her appearance. "At first I thought she was a nun, from her black dress and close cap," this lady wrote. A moment later she realized, "It is Miss Nightingale!" She continued, "I was glad not to be obliged to speak just then, for I felt quite dumb as I looked at her wasted figure and the short brown hair combed over her forehead like a child's." The lady used this brief pause to give Nightingale a good once-over. "Her face is long and thin, but this may be from recent illness and great fatigue," she noted. "She looks like a quiet, persevering, orderly, ladylike woman."

Nightingale's perseverance was about to pay off. In January 1856, Colonel John Lefroy, scientific advisor to the secretary of state for war, completed a months-long investigation of nursing in the military hospitals. He met with Nightingale and learned of all she had accomplished. He also went to the Crimean Peninsula and observed Bridgeman's nurses at work. Based on what he had seen, he recommended that all nurses in the war zone take orders from one person. He made sure that "the rightful position of Miss Nightingale" was written into the army's general orders. This meant that Nightingale had what she had long wanted: oversight of every nurse in every army hospital in the war zone.

The next time she visited the Crimean Peninsula, the army provided a mule-drawn covered wagon to take her from place to place. As she went from one hospital to another, she met with the nurses and observed them at work. At Balaclava's General Hospital, Nightingale informed Mother Bridgeman of the new order. Bridgeman resigned rather than submit to Nightingale's authority, and she and the Sisters of Charity sailed for home.

Days later, the fighting nations signed a treaty in Paris. The war that had cost a quarter million lives ended with no clear winner. The Russians returned occupied territory to the Ottoman Empire, but they still craved power in the region and in a few years they would try once more to gain it.

Florence Nightingale hardly noticed the coming of peace because ailing soldiers still needed care. Much work had to be done to bring the hospitals on the Crimean Peninsula up to her high standards. The staffs and patients lacked supplies, the wards were filthy, and rodents scurried about at night. In a letter to her sister, Nightingale described killing a plump rat with a broom handle. She asked Parthenope, "Would not you like to see me hunting rats like a terrier-dog? Me!"

CHAPTER 9

Nightingale Power

BACK in Scutari, as patients and nurses said their goodbyes and left, the Barrack Hospital grew strangely quiet. "The last of our Invalids go home today," Nightingale wrote on July 23, 1856. She bade a silent farewell to the twenty-two thousand British soldiers who had died in the war. "I have been such a bad mother to you, to come home and leave you lying in your Crimean graves," she whispered. She reflected on how she had seen three-quarters of the men in eight regiments wiped out by disease in just six months. With the British public caught up in the joy of peace, "Who thinks of that now?" she asked herself.

At the end of July, Florence and her aunt left Scutari, the dirty, ravaged port that had been Florence's home for nearly two years. Mai Smith warned Mr. and Mrs. Nightingale about what to expect when they next saw their daughter. Florence was weaker than she might at first appear. "I see her at times when she seems hardly able to walk across the room from fatigue & deeply depressed in spirits," Smith wrote.

Hoping to avoid a grand, noisy welcome, the pair traveled as a mother and daughter, Mrs. and Miss Smith. They parted in London, and Flo took a train to Derbyshire. She then walked the mile and a half from the station to Lea Hurst. Her family knew she was back only when their housekeeper looked out a window and spotted her passing through the back gate. Florence entered the house quietly, "like a bird," Parthenope said. Her return was "a blessing," Mrs. Nightingale thought, "for which we cannot be too thankful." "A little tinkle of the small church bell on the hills, and a thanksgiving prayer at the little chapel next day" were all that marked her homecoming, according to Parthe.

A few weeks later, Parthe reported to Liz Herbert that Flo showed little improvement. Illness had sapped her strength, "& I cannot believe that she will live long," Parthe wrote. "I see she does not think so herself, not that she ever says so." Rest was impossible for Florence, because so many matters demanded her attention. Once word that she was home had spread, gifts and letters poured in as never before. She

Chef Alexis Soyer had the covered wagon from Nightingale's final trip to the Crimean Peninsula transported to England. It was later put on display.

Lea Hurst Sept /56
A troublesome litter.

Before setting out for home, Nightingale had sent three youths to England. They carried a letter to her family with instructions to make sure these "Crimean treasures" received schooling. The first lad was a sailor named William Jones who had lost a leg in the war; Nightingale would later find him work. The second was the loyal drummer boy, Thomas. The third was a twelve-year-old Russian orphan, Peter Grillage, who had been captured and taken to one of the hospitals. He later became a servant at Embley. The boys brought with them a fourth treasure, an enormous puppy named Roosh. Some soldiers had discovered Roosh in the streets of Scutari, abandoned and starving, and had given him to Nightingale. He too found a home on the Nightingale estates.

spent hours responding to strangers who were requesting everything from money to a donkey, and to ordinary citizens sending their thanks.

She also pondered what to do with the rest of her life. Living quietly at home was out of the question for a woman who felt called to serve. She could open a training school for nurses; in fact, some of London's leading citizens had established a fund expressly for this purpose. Donations arrived from all over England. Wealthy families made large contributions; churches took up collections; soldiers gave what they could. The famed Swedish opera singer Jenny Lind raised nearly nineteen hundred pounds at a benefit concert in London. By summer 1856, the Nightingale Fund held more than forty-four thousand pounds, an amount worth millions of U.S. dollars today.

A more urgent project than a school, in Nightingale's opinion, was improving health care in the army. She thought of the suffering men she had encountered when she reached Scutari in 1854. In her mind she could see these "living skeletons" covered with fleas and lice; she recalled them lying on the hospital floor with open, oozing sores and passing too soon into death. She vowed to make sure that British soldiers never again endured such shameful neglect. "I stand at the Altar of the murdered men and while I live I fight their cause," she proclaimed.

Late that summer Florence heard from Sir James Clark, the royal physician who had treated Parthenope during her time of mental distress. He invited Florence to visit his family's home in Scotland. Queen Victoria's Scottish retreat, Balmoral Castle, was nearby, and the queen wished to meet Florence and hear firsthand about the military hospitals. For Florence, this was an opportunity not to be missed. She needed the support of powerful people if she hoped to improve army health care. She went to Scotland with her father in mid-September.

Balmoral Castle turned out to be a strange place. It was famously cold and drafty, which bothered everyone but the queen. The rooms had been decorated according to Victoria's peculiar taste. She liked Scotland so much that she had the floors, furniture, windows, and walls covered in Scottish plaids. "The effect is not very pretty," grumbled one guest who had grown cranky from lack of warmth. The men and boys in the royal family wore kilts while at Balmoral, and the short, plump queen spoke with a Scottish burr when she was there.

Victoria had expected the famous nurse to be a tiresome do-gooder, "a rather cold, stiff, reserved person," as she wrote in her journal. Instead she met someone "gentle, pleasing and engaging, most ladylike and so clever, clear and comprehensive in her views of everything." Victoria continued, "Her mind is solely and entirely taken up with the *one* object to which she has sacrificed her health and devoted herself like a saint. . . . Such a character," noted the queen, "is in a woman most rare and extraordinary!" Victoria concluded her description by observing that Nightingale "must have been very pretty but now she looks very thin and careworn."

As Victoria was sizing up her guest, Nightingale formed her own opinion of the queen. Victoria, she later told a friend, was the least self-reliant person she had ever met. The woman who ruled the world's greatest empire constantly turned to her husband, German-born Prince Albert, for reassurance. In Albert, Nightingale saw a man for whom life was a burden. He looked, she thought, "like a person who wanted to die." Nightingale had seen enough of death to spot someone who had lost the will to live. Sure enough, Albert's health would soon decline. He would die young, at forty-two, in 1861.

The two women had a long talk about the shocking mismanagement that had caused such distress in the army camps and hospitals. Victoria agreed with Nightingale

This photograph of Nightingale was taken soon after she returned to England.

THE QUEEN & PRINCE CONSORT.

Queen Victoria adored her husband, Prince Albert, and consulted him on matters of state. Florence Nightingale thought, however, that the queen lacked self-confidence and depended too heavily on her husband's guidance.

on the need for an inquiry and for reform. Although queen, she had no authority to change national policy; that power belonged to government ministers and Parliament. Victoria could only offer her opinion and try to persuade. She asked Nightingale to remain in Scotland and speak to the secretary of state for war, Lord Panmure, who would arrive on October 5. Nightingale stayed in obedience to her queen, but she doubted that Panmure would be of much help. His office had been responsible for the inhumane treatment of the soldiers. She expected that he would try to avoid any embarrassing reminders of what had gone wrong.

To Nightingale's surprise, Panmure was open to working with her for change. He asked her to review the plans for the first general military hospital in Britain, which was being built on England's southern coast. He agreed to appoint a royal commission to look into the problems in the army hospitals during the war. And he requested that Nightingale write a report containing all her observations of wartime medical care and her suggestions for improvement.

Hundreds of hours of work lay ahead, but Florence Nightingale liked nothing better. She could hardly wait to take on her newest challenge, despite being ill. She announced to her family, "For the next three or four months I shall have business (imposed on me by Panmure) which will require hard work & time spent in London & elsewhere to see men & institutions." Wanting to be near the offices of government, she moved into a suite at London's Burlington Hotel. There she had a sitting room on the lower level and a bedroom above. The rooms were fine for holding meetings and doing her work, even if they were hot and airless in summer. She would come to call her suite at the Burlington the "Little War Office."

Nightingale preferred to work outside the public eye. Not only did she hate publicity, but illness often confined her to bed. She held no official position and drew no salary, yet she was to have an enormous impact on the actions of government. This influence—unprecedented at a time when women could not even vote—became known as "the Nightingale power."

Mrs. Nightingale and Parthe quickly installed themselves in Florence's sitting room. Fanny Nightingale greeted callers while Parthe wrote letters and did other clerical work. Meanwhile, Florence tackled the important tasks from her bedroom. Her illness left Florence with little patience, and it irked her to think that her mother and sister were downstairs playing at being busy. She remembered how they had tried to stop her from pursuing nursing just a few years earlier. "There was nothing different except my popularity," she knew. "What have mother & sister ever done for me? They like my glory," she complained in a private note to herself.

Her mother and sister did savor the attention they received as relatives of the renowned Florence Nightingale, but they also helped her a great deal. And Mrs. Nightingale wanted to be nearby because she worried about Florence's health. Some days Florence spent twenty hours working. If Fanny Nightingale woke at 1:30 a.m., she saw a light still burning in Florence's room. Florence "so entirely forgets herself that she would not eat at all unless the food were put before her," Fanny noted in despair.

When Florence's Crimean fever flared up in August 1857, causing her heart to pound and her spirits to sink, her family was concerned but hardly surprised. Her doctor ordered her to the town of Malvern, a popular health spa, for a water cure, and Mai Smith went along to help care for her. Florence would have more attacks of illness in the decades to come. Each time, sure she was about to die, she wrote out her will. Yet she always pulled through, and she did a remarkable amount of work despite her chronic ill health.

THIS IS THE WAY WE ARE TREATED, AS IF WE WERE GARDEN SHRUBS.

Nº 8

A patient undergoing a water cure suffers through a cold shower in this 1869 cartoon.

During the months she spent writing her report, Nightingale drew on the careful notes she had kept while in Scutari. Her evidence showed that the army had caused thousands of its soldiers to die needlessly from disease and exposure. "Our soldiers enlist to death in the barracks," she declared in a passage that would be widely printed in newspapers. In the future the army needed to outfit its fighting men in warm clothes, give them nourishing food, shelter them against the weather, and keep their quarters and hospital wards clean and well ventilated.

She had help compiling the report from her dear friend Sidney Herbert. The two met often at Herbert's home or at the Little War Office. They sent notes to each other when apart, asking questions and sharing ideas. Nightingale also had help from John Sutherland, the Scottish doctor who had gone to Scutari with the sanitary commission and who had since become her physician and friend. Dr. William Farr was another member of her team. He was an expert in medical statistics who had spent twenty years gathering data on disease and death in England. Farr had studied so many epidemics that if a new one erupted in humans

Dr. William Farr was a leader in the field of medical statistics. He advised Nightingale when she was organizing data for her report on the health of the British army.

or livestock, he could draw a curve that would accurately show the rapid rise in cases as the disease spread and the more dramatic drop in new infections once the epidemic reached its peak.

Nightingale was as tough on the men as she was on herself and constantly drove them to work harder and longer. If Herbert protested that he was weary and unwell, she told him that his ailments were imagined. If Sutherland spent too much time tending his garden, she found ways to draw him away. Once, when he had excused himself from a work session, Nightingale reacted by fainting. The loyal doctor hurried to the Burlington Hotel as soon as a messenger brought him the news. He humbly apologized for causing her distress. Sutherland let Nightingale pull his strings because he felt honored to collaborate with her. "Nobody who has not worked with her daily could know her, could have an idea of her strength and clearness of mind, her extraordinary powers joined with her benevolence of spirit," he said.

The investigative group that Panmure had promised, the Royal Commission on the Health of the Army, began holding hearings in May 1857. Nightingale had recommended Sidney Herbert to serve as its chair, and he agreed to do so, despite his claims of illness. Nightingale provided the commission with data on soldiers' health and hospital conditions during the Crimean War, although she refused to testify in person.

The commissioners also looked into the well-being of British soldiers stationed at home while the nation was at peace. As Herbert and the others waded through piles of paper and visited army barracks and hospitals, they discovered something startling. The death rate for soldiers in peacetime was twice as high as the rate among civilians. This knowledge was especially alarming because the army allowed only healthy men to enlist. What were the causes? Crowding, drunkenness, and poor sanitation, including defective sewers, the commission reported. Many of these deaths could easily be prevented.

Meanwhile, Nightingale's report, titled *Notes on Matters Affecting the Health, Efficiency and Hospital Administration of the British Army*, was finished in September. It was an armful, more than eight hundred pages long and full of statistics and numerical tables. Nightingale's use of statistics to reveal trends in health care was altogether new. Her tables and graphs let lawmakers see at a glance the problems

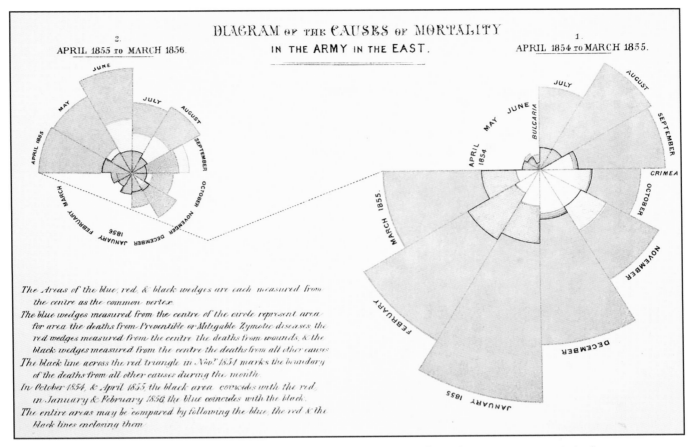

DIAGRAM OF THE CAUSES OF MORTALITY
IN THE ARMY IN THE EAST.

2.
APRIL 1855 TO MARCH 1856.

1.
APRIL 1854 TO MARCH 1855.

The Areas of the blue, red, & black wedges are each measured from
the centre as the common vertex.
The blue wedges measured from the centre of the circle represent area
for area the deaths from Preventible or Mitigable Zymotic diseases, the
red wedges measured from the centre the deaths from wounds, & the
black wedges measured from the centre the deaths from all other causes.
The black line across the red triangle in Nov.r 1854 marks the boundary
of the deaths from all other causes during the month.
In October 1854, & April 1855, the black area coincides with the red,
in January & February 1856, the blue coincides with the black.
The entire areas may be compared by following the blue, the red, & the
black lines enclosing them.

In her report, Florence Nightingale pioneered the use of graphs to present statistical information on health trends. By looking at her pie graphs, government officials could clearly see how many more soldiers died from preventable causes than from battlefield wounds.

she had identified. This innovative work earned Nightingale admission to the Royal Statistical Society in 1858. Her study of mathematics as a young woman was serving her well.

Panmure, hoping to avoid the public's wrath, was already taking steps toward reform. He had created committees to improve army buildings, compile statistics on soldiers' health, make over the army medical department, and establish an army medical school. Overworked Sidney Herbert agreed to chair them all.

As he had promised, Panmure sent Nightingale the plans for the Royal Victoria Military Hospital, which was being built in the small town of Netley, near

Southampton. Nightingale was dismayed to see that its layout was outdated. The architect had designed a building that would look beautiful when viewed from the water. But the finished hospital would pack patients too close together, with too little breathing space. Nightingale advised the army to build a modern hospital like the one that was going up in Paris. This hospital was going to feature spacious pavilions, or wings. Windows could be opened on both sides of a pavilion to let in healthful fresh air.

Construction had already begun on the hospital at Netley, though. Switching to a pavilion design at this point would be expensive, and it would make the army look foolish, so Panmure rejected Nightingale's suggestions. Unwilling to be defeated, Nightingale appealed to Lord Palmerston, the prime minister. After weighing all the pros and cons, Palmerston determined that scrapping the project and starting over would cost too much money. He did order some improvements that Nightingale had suggested, such as wider corridors and more windows.

After she returned from Malvern, Florence turned her mother and sister out of the Burlington Hotel. Mai Smith came to take their place and deal with Florence's whims and complaints. Some days Florence was so cross that she refused to see callers, even close friends like Clarkey. She was saving her energy for work, she said. Sounds set her nerves on edge. A carriage rumbling in the street, music — the source hardly mattered. Noise was noise.

Her days of traveling and touring hospitals were over. From this time on she lived as an invalid and often worked from her bed. She quit going to church and conducted her own religious services in her room. After visiting Embley in 1858, she stayed away for eight years. She would not see her cherished Lea Hurst for a decade. "I fear Florence's power of work & therefore hold on life is disappearing from month to month," her father wrote. Others in the family agreed. In fact, belief in the nearness of Florence's death was the reason Mai Smith neglected her own family to serve her niece.

Around this time an older gentleman, Sir Harry Verney, began calling at the Burlington Hotel. His late wife had wanted their daughter Emily, now fifteen, to meet the heroic Miss Nightingale, and he hoped to make her wish come true. Sir Harry saw that Florence was too ill to devote time to a young lady, but he visited the Nightingale family and noticed Florence's sister. He had been lonely since his wife's death, and there was something about Parthenope that reminded him of her. Once he got to know Parthe, he grew determined to make her the second Lady Verney.

Sir Harry became a frequent caller at Embley. "He woos her like a soldier in haste as if he was just setting off for the wars," Mrs. Nightingale commented. By spring 1858 Sir Harry had won Parthe's heart, and she agreed to marry him. The wedding took place quietly, on June 22. Florence was too ill to attend, but she sent this message to her sister: "God bless you,

Parthenope Nightingale found happiness as Lady Verney.

my dear Pop—and take my blessing and my best thoughts with you on your marriage day."

Florence liked Sir Harry, who became her friend and political advisor. Sir Harry served in Parliament and owned a historic mansion called Claydon House. It gladdened Florence to know that with a wealthy husband, Parthe would be financially secure for the rest of her life. But at thirty-nine Parthe was unlikely to bear a son to be heir to the Nightingale estate. Florence and her mother would still face an uncertain future if William Nightingale were to die.

A younger man started stopping by the Burlington Hotel too. Arthur Clough was married to Florence's cousin Blanche, Mai Smith's oldest daughter. Arthur wrote poetry and worked in the government's education department. Although his wife delighted in her home and children like a conventional Victorian lady, he believed that women, like men, should do work that fulfilled them. As he wrote in one poem, "It is beautiful only to do the thing we are meant for."

Clough also believed that the human heart found comfort in simple, useful work. Once he discovered that he could be of service to Florence, who was doing so much good, he became devoted to her. He mailed parcels for her and carried messages—no errand was too small. With Arthur there to check timetables and help her into train cars, Florence took restful trips to places outside London, where she

Arthur Hugh Clough, poet and husband of Nightingale's cousin Blanche Smith, was devoted to Florence Nightingale.

stayed in rented houses. Sometimes on these journeys, if she felt well enough, she went for donkey rides.

Arthur Clough never rested. He left the education department by four o'clock each afternoon and hurried over to the Burlington Hotel, where he worked with Florence late into the night. He helped ready her government report, proofreading pages and dealing with the printer. In the same way, he aided with the articles, pamphlets, and other books that Florence wrote during this busy time. He asked for nothing in return, but in 1859 Florence gave Arthur and Blanche five hundred pounds toward the purchase of a home for their growing family. Their daughter Florence—one of the many English girls named after Nightingale—was a year old. A son, Arthur, was soon to be born.

She also made Clough secretary of the Nightingale Fund, a post for which she paid him a hundred pounds a year. People were starting to ask what was happening to the money they had donated at the end of the war. It was time for Florence to apply Nightingale power to the next important project: the long-awaited nursing school.

Chapter 10

Maid of All Work

THE Nightingale School of Nursing welcomed its first students in July 1860. They were all women, because Florence Nightingale believed that nursing was a woman's profession. Their ages ranged from twenty-five to thirty-five. Nightingale expected them to be of good character, to be "sober, honest, truthful, trustworthy, punctual, quiet and orderly, cleanly and neat, patient, cheerful, and kindly." She would settle for nothing less. The school was housed in London's St. Thomas's Hospital, an old establishment. St. Thomas's was clean and well run, and its governors, who included Prince Albert, were among Nightingale's admirers.

Upon arriving, the eleven students—called probationers—received their uniforms: plain brown dresses and white aprons and caps. Thanks to the Nightingale Fund, they paid no tuition. During training, they received ten pounds' wages and room and board.

The probationers were making nursing history. For the first time anywhere, women were learning to be nurses in a nonreligious school. They were acquiring all the skills a good nurse needed, from dressing wounds to applying leeches. The probationers received instruction from trained, experienced nursing sisters and attended lectures on disease given by physicians. They learned to feed patients who were too sick to feed themselves and to shift patients too weak to move. They made bandages, kept the wards clean, and observed operations. They also learned some Latin, the language used to print directions on medicine bottles. After a year of training, the probationers spent three more years working at St. Thomas's or another hospital. They would emerge at the end of that time as practiced, professional nurses.

The hospital's matron, or head nurse, was Sarah Elizabeth Wardroper. She supervised the probationers just as Nightingale had overseen the nurses at Scutari. Wardroper had no formal training, but she had worked hard for many years, learning as she went along. She had built a reputation for careful, competent nursing at St. Thomas's.

Nightingale was too ill and in too much pain to teach the probationers herself. She advised the school's faculty and kept track of the probationers' progress from her bed. She drew up a form for the matron to fill out, assessing each probationer's honesty, punctuality, and neatness. Nightingale's male colleagues, especially Arthur Clough, took care of business matters for the school.

St. Thomas's Hospital had one drawback: it was slated to be torn down to make room for a railroad line. Within two years of the school's opening, the hospital relocated to temporary quarters in what used to be a music hall and zoo while a new building went up outside the city. Physicians treated cholera patients in the old giraffe house; medical students dissected cadavers in the former elephant house. And the probationers continued to learn.

Just a few years had passed since her return from Scutari, but Nightingale could take pride in a string of accomplishments. The nursing school was up and running. The nation's soldiers were enjoying better health. Army leaders knew this was true, because thanks to Nightingale and William Farr, they had learned to keep careful statistics. An army medical college had opened at Chatham, in southeast England. It trained military doctors in the latest techniques for treating gunshot wounds and tropical diseases, and it schooled them in sanitation. Also, books by Florence Nightingale were educating health professionals and ordinary readers.

The probationers ate their meals together in a dining room at St. Thomas's Hospital.

In *Notes on Hospitals,* published in 1859, Nightingale explained how a hospital's design could either make patients sicker or help them get well. Diseases spread in crowded, poorly ventilated hospital wards, she wrote, because the air grew toxic. It could "poison the blood not only of the sick . . . but also of the medical attendants and nurses." She still held tightly to the miasma theory and rejected the idea that a disease could be contagious. "There is no such thing as 'contagion,'" she wrote. She went so far as to claim that with "proper sanitary precautions"—with fresh air, light, cleanliness, and ample space—"diseases reputed to be the most 'infectious' may be treated in wards among other sick without any danger." Her reasoning was flawed, but the measures Nightingale recommended did promote good health. Her book confirmed her reputation as an expert on hospitals.

Nightingale wrote another popular book, *Notes on Nursing,* for people who were caring for the sick at home. Again she based her advice on the miasma theory. The sufferings of the sick "are very often not symptoms of the disease at all," she taught, "but of something quite different—of the want of fresh air, or of light, or of warmth, or of quiet, or of cleanliness, or of punctuality and care in the administration of diet." In *Notes on Nursing* Nightingale brought readers inside the narrow, fretful world of the sick. "The very walls of their sick rooms seem hung with their cares," she wrote. "The ghosts of their troubles haunt their beds."

This slender, easy-to-read book contained chapters on practical subjects such as food for invalids, proper bedding, cleanliness, and noise. For readers today, it offers an intriguing peek inside the English Victorian home. It reveals, for example, that foul sewer odors seeped through pipes into even the finest houses. "I have met just as strong a stream of sewer air coming up the back staircase of a grand London house from the sink, as I have ever met at Scutari," Nightingale wrote. Within two months, the public snatched up fifteen thousand copies of *Notes on Nursing*.

Nightingale printed just a few copies of *Suggestions for Thought*, her book about religion. She remained devoutly Christian, although her faith differed from the religion that was practiced in most English churches, which relied on prayer. She called for faith in God that was based on action. "His scheme for us was not that He should give us what we ask for, but that mankind should obtain it for mankind," she wrote. She questioned some Christian teachings, asking whether miracles described in the Bible had ever actually happened and whether God really condemned some souls to hell. It was high time for people to read the Bible with a questioning mind, she stated.

Suggestions for Thought also contained an essay Nightingale wrote about women. She titled it "Cassandra," after a woman in Greek mythology with the gift of prophecy and the curse of not having her prophecies believed. In Nightingale's opinion, many Englishwomen were nineteenth-century Cassandras, endowed with potential but condemned to live idle lives. The women of her day endured mental and emotional starvation, she wrote: "no food for our heads, no food for our hearts, no food for our activity." She commented, "One would think we had no heads nor hearts." Girls were trained from an early age to stifle their dreams, to occupy themselves with family, husband, and home. "Awake, ye women, all ye that sleep, awake!" Nightingale called out from the page. "The time is come when women must do something more than the 'domestic hearth.'"

One reason Nightingale was able to achieve so much is that another woman had been tending her domestic hearth. In summer 1860, after spending nearly three years at Florence's beck and call, Mai Smith went home. She was sixty-two years old, her joints ached, her family missed her, and Florence apparently was not about to die. Florence reacted bitterly, refusing to see things from Mai's point of view. She took the departure personally, as a rejection of everything she stood for. Flo's cousin Hilary Bonham Carter, who had never married, took Mai's place at the Burlington Hotel. Still, Florence stayed angry at her aunt for years to come. Her friend Clarkey worried that illness and isolation were affecting Florence's mind.

Mai Smith's son-in-law Arthur Clough remained faithful, but overwork was destroying his health. At Christmas 1859, he came down with scarlet fever. In the years before this streptococcal infection could be treated with antibiotics, it often progressed to rheumatic fever, which can damage the heart. This is what happened to Clough. Months went by, and his weakness lingered. He took a leave of absence from his job at the education department and went to Malvern for a water cure, but he came home not much better. Hoping that travel would restore his health, he journeyed to the Isle of Wight, off England's southern coast, and to the Pyrenees Mountains in France.

Sidney Herbert was failing too. A year after Arthur Clough got sick, Herbert learned that he had diabetes and kidney disease. This was not the kind of news Nightingale wanted to hear. Not only was Herbert a close friend, but he was a key ally in her work on behalf of soldiers, one she had no intention of losing. "You know I don't believe in fatal diseases," she scoffed. She gave Herbert pep talks, reminding him that she worked hard despite being an invalid. As a nurse, she advised that "sleep, fresh air, regular food: these are the three great medicines." And she pushed him to keep toiling.

Herbert came to see her on July 9, 1861. Thin and trembling, he had trouble climbing the stairs at the Burlington Hotel. When he told her that he was going to a spa for a water cure, she accused him of throwing away his opportunities. Impatiently she sent him off. Less than a month later, Sidney Herbert, age fifty, was dead. Liz Herbert wrote down his last words: "Poor Florence! Our joint work unfinished."

"Grief fills up the room," Florence wrote, adding, "[It] eats and sleeps and wakes with me." Too ill to attend the funeral, she mourned privately at home. "I am his real widow," she wrote to Clarkey. Although she had never loved Sidney in a romantic way, she had lost a partner. She had been hard on him, she admitted to herself, and she vowed never to forget his "angelic temper." She authored a pamphlet in which she praised his efforts to prevent disease and death in the army, whether at war or at peace. "He constantly kept before him as the great object of his official life," she wrote, "to increase the efficiency, improve the position, and preserve the health of the British soldier." She continued, "He will be remembered chiefly as the first war minister who ever seriously set himself the task of saving life."

Liz Herbert remained Florence's friend, but when Arthur Clough died a few months later, his widow turned against her cousin Florence. It was "all the money-making and working for F. Nightingale which had worn him out," insisted Blanche Smith Clough. Florence felt hurt that Blanche and other family members showed her no sympathy. She had loved Arthur too. In fact, she compared her relationship with Arthur to the loving friendship of David and Jonathan, whose story is told in the Bible. When Jonathan is killed in battle, David mourns deeply. "Oh Jonathan, my brother Jonathan, my love to thee was very great," Florence wrote, lamenting the loss of Arthur Clough. She felt a kinship to Queen Victoria, who lost her husband, Prince Albert, in December 1861.

Florence Nightingale soon left the Burlington Hotel. Too many reminders of departed friends filled its rooms. If she looked out the window, she recalled the many times she had seen Sidney Herbert walk down the street. For a few years she moved from one rented London dwelling to another, each time having all her papers and government reports hauled after her. None of these places suited her, so in 1865 her father purchased a home where she could settle down, at 35 South Street. It was "truly a beautiful house," Florence said. From her bedroom windows she looked out on Hyde Park, one of London's largest and prettiest green spaces. She began to take in cats. Tom, Tib, Gladstone, Mr. Muff—she always had a few. She let them walk all over her bed and leave paw prints on her papers while she scolded her maids for being slatternly. Servants could never keep the rooms clean enough to meet Nightingale's high standard of hygiene. She gave one maid a tongue-lashing for putting the chamber pot on a chair, on top of Nightingale's lace cap.

Also in 1865, Hilary Bonham Carter, Florence's cousin and friend since childhood, died of cancer at age forty-four. Florence once more expressed her sadness in a letter to Clarkey. "The golden bowl is broken," she wrote, "and it was the purest gold."

New friends eased Florence's loneliness. Among them was the Reverend Benjamin Jowett, a brilliant professor of classical Greek. Jowett wrote to Nightingale after reading *Suggestions for Thought* and soon became a frequent visitor. The two could talk for hours about religion and society's ills. Jowett asked her to read drafts of his sermons, and he showed her his translation of Plato, his most important scholarly work. Like Nightingale, Jowett was happiest when he was busy. "Little time is lost through ill-health," he told his classes, "though much is lost through idleness." He had a wide forehead, befitting a man with such a powerful brain, but his smile was playful, even childlike. One of his students remarked that his high-pitched voice sounded like a "cherubic chirp," especially "when he was at his ease and at his best."

Jowett could say things to Nightingale that would have drawn her anger coming from other people. For example, he cautioned her to be conscious of her affliction, as it "at times clouds your mind—and takes away self control." He persuaded Nightingale to make amends to her cousin Blanche and aunt Mai. He befriended Fanny and William Nightingale and spent time at Lea Hurst. He stood beside the river Derwent and walked in the parkland so he could describe these favorite spots to Florence when he returned.

By the time she met Jowett, Nightingale was immersed in a giant project, improving health in India, much of which was then a British colony. Great Britain had been stationing large numbers of soldiers in India following uprisings in the 1850s. Their living conditions were at least as bad as those Nightingale had encountered during the Crimean War. Men slept in crowded quarters in intense heat, close to latrines and garbage heaps. They were attacked nightly by bedbugs and fleas. Too many died from unexplained

Benjamin Jowett became Nightingale's friend in later life. An acquaintance claimed that Jowett had wanted Florence Nightingale to be his wife, but there is no evidence that he proposed marriage to her.

fevers, hepatitis, heatstroke, diarrhea, and cholera. Cholera was so rampant at some army bases that newly arriving soldiers were warned they would never leave alive. Nightingale was too sick to travel to India and assess the situation herself, so she wrote letters to base commanders there, asking about the men's diet, clothing, and medical care, and about sanitation and climate.

Conditions were dismal for India's two hundred and forty million civilians, too. Nightingale wanted a public-health plan that would benefit everyone in India, one that provided clean water, sewage systems, and doctors. She also called for irrigation to protect crops in times of drought. Many farmers depended on monsoon rains to water their fields, and if the monsoon failed to come, their crops withered in the sun. This is what happened in 1860 and 1861, when two million people starved to death in India's northwestern provinces.

Nightingale wrote pamphlets and newspaper articles informing the British public about India's needs. She put together a health-education booklet that was to be translated into the local languages of India. She used her Nightingale power to have Parliament appoint a royal commission to look into sanitary conditions in the army in India. Its report, published in 1863, was two thousand pages long.

In his playful way, Benjamin Jowett teased Nightingale about all that she did. He dubbed her "Florence the First, Empress of Scavengers, Queen of Nurses, Reverend Mother Superior of the British Army, Governess of the Governor of India." Serious Florence corrected him, saying that she was merely a "Maid of all (dirty) work."

Sir John Lawrence, the queen's representative in India, was eager to put Nightingale's plans into action. He created sanitary commissions in three separate regions, and they began making improvements in 1864. But the army had only so much money, and India was vast, covering 1.4 million square miles in the 1800s. It had swamps, deserts, forests, mountains, and four thousand miles of coastline. Although Nightingale's dream of reforming public health in such a large, geographically diverse place would never be fully realized, she worked for decades to achieve it.

Nightingale also found ways to serve humanity closer to home. In the nineteenth century, British law required people who needed public aid to enter workhouses (also

DAILY MEANS OF OCCUPATION AND AMUSEMENT. INDIA *passim*.

British soldiers in India relax in their barracks. Nightingale thought that boredom contributed to alcohol abuse and related health problems among the men.

called houses of industry). In these large institutions, they received food and beds in exchange for their labor. Workhouse inmates broke up stones for road-making. They ground corn into meal, chopped wood, and grew vegetables to feed themselves and their fellow paupers. In some workhouses, people pulverized animal bones for fertilizer. In others, they picked apart old ropes with their fingers. The loose fiber, called oakum, would be mixed with tar to make a waterproof coating for the hulls of ships.

One hundred and fifty thousand people lived in Britain's houses of industry in the 1860s. Many were healthy men and women of working age, but others were old or very young, and up to a third were ill or disabled. Workhouses had infirmaries for the sick but no trained nurses to staff them. Very often the task of nursing was left to women living in the institution. Unschooled in health care, they were as likely to harm the patients as help them. Ill or well, inmates slept on filthy linens, sometimes three to a bed. They lacked clean water for washing and often went days without breathing fresh air. Town and city leaders wanted workhouse life to be harsh, because they believed that paupers were lazy. If conditions were too pleasant, they thought, poor men and women would never seek paying jobs.

Nightingale believed that workhouses punished people for being poor when these individuals ought to be receiving society's help. She wanted to reform the entire national system for housing the poor, but she focused on one aspect of the problem: getting trained nurses into workhouse infirmaries. She asked her fellow Britons to put aside their bias, especially when a pauper got sick. "From that moment he ceases to be a pauper and becomes brother to the best of us," she wrote, "and as a brother he should be cared for."

This work began in the northern port of Liverpool with help from a wealthy merchant who wanted to use his money to do good. In 1859, when William Rathbone's wife was dying, he had been grateful for the care she received from a nurse. He wished for the poor to have skillful nursing when they were sick too. Nightingale selected twelve nurses who had trained at the Nightingale School to staff the infirmary at the Brownlow Hill Workhouse in Liverpool. On May 16, 1865, the women began their work. The nurse Nightingale placed in charge was Agnes Jones, whom Sarah Wardroper had singled out as showing exceptional promise.

Eighteen months later, a government inspector visited the infirmary at Brownlow Hill. "Great care and attention appear to be paid to the sick, who seem to be fully supplied with everything that is essential to their condition," he reported. "The cleanliness, neatness, and order of the wards cannot be excelled." He saw separate wards for women and men, and others devoted to surgical cases, women giving birth, and cholera patients. Yet "in most of these wards," the inspector continued, "the beds are too close together." Many were "seriously defective in regard to ventilation; some of them may be described as being in this respect in a bad, and some in a *very* bad state." Clearly, more work needed to be done.

Acting on advice from Florence Nightingale, Rathbone founded a nursing school in Liverpool. Soon the city was divided into nursing districts, each overseen by a

Crowding was a way of life in Britain's workhouses.

female superintendent. Other cities adopted Liverpool's model, leading to a national system of district nursing for the poor. Also, Parliament was persuaded in 1867 to amend the poor law, ensuring that workhouse residents needing hospital care would receive it. The law removed children from workhouses and placed them in asylums.

Thanks to the hard work of Agnes Jones and her nurses, William Rathbone, Florence Nightingale, and others, Britain's poor were enjoying better health. Rathbone was so grateful for Nightingale's help that for the rest of his life, he made sure she always had fresh flowers in her room.

CHAPTER 11

A Noble Life

IN the world beyond Florence Nightingale's flower-scented room, scientists were learning more about disease. Through experiments conducted in the early 1860s, a French chemist and biologist named Louis Pasteur had demonstrated that illnesses could be contagious. He proved that microorganisms caused many of them, including cholera.

An English surgeon, Joseph Lister, applied Pasteur's findings to the problem of infections in open wounds. Lister suspected that it was not bad air that caused surgical incisions and other wounds to fester, as they often did. Rather, it was contact with minute particles, "the germs of various low forms of life." Lister tried cleaning wounds and treating them with carbolic acid, or phenol. He was so sure this weak acid was a good germ killer that he sprayed it in the operating rooms at the Glasgow Royal Infirmary in Scotland, where he worked. He also wiped his surgical instruments with it.

Other physicians made fun of Lister's efforts. "Where are these little beasts?" asked Dr. John Hughes Bennett, a professor in Edinburgh. "Show them to us, and we shall believe in them." Lister had the last laugh, though. After he started using carbolic acid in 1865, the death rate among surgical patients at his hospital dropped markedly.

As someone who believed in progress, Florence Nightingale gradually came to accept the germ theory of disease. By the 1870s, probationers at the Nightingale School of Nursing were learning Lister's antiseptic methods.

The new St. Thomas's Hospital opened in 1871, across the river Thames from Parliament. It had been built with many wings, or pavilions, branching out from a

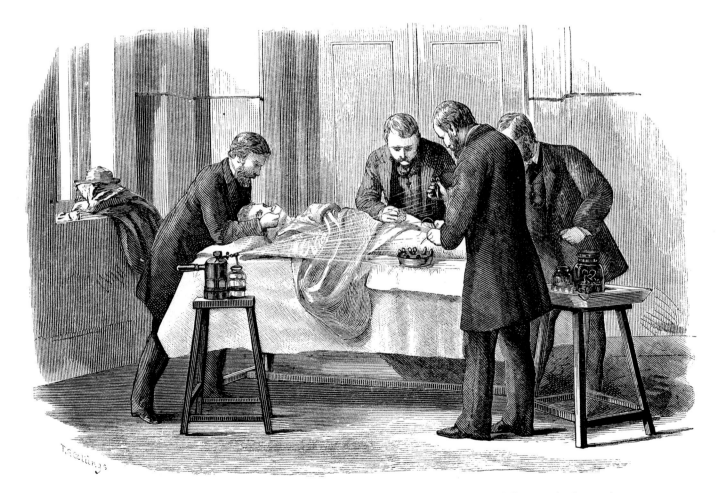

Surgeons operating in 1882 follow Lister's antiseptic method. Germ-killing carbolic acid bathes the doctors' hands and instruments and the patient's open wound.

central corridor. The design gave all the wards windows to let in light and fresh air. "The principal feature of the place, however, is its astounding bigness," remarked a writer for the *Lancet*, Britain's leading medical journal. St. Thomas's was so big, with so many long corridors, that the writer hoped each doctor's patients were grouped together. If they were scattered throughout the hospital, it would be "a task beyond even medical long-suffering and endurance" for the doctor to see them all. The Nightingale School, still housed in the hospital, was sending trained nurses overseas, to Australia and Canada, to meet needs there.

Florence Nightingale continued to monitor the school. Beginning in 1872, she wrote yearly letters to the probationers that Sir Harry Verney read aloud to them. In these letters Nightingale spoke often of religion, reminding the women to make God their first thought in the morning and their last thought at night. She advised them to keep on learning throughout their careers and to serve as examples to others. What a student nurse needed most was "to have high principles at the bottom of all," she wrote. Year after year, she reminded the probationers of those principles: kindness, sympathy, consideration, trustworthiness, and obedience.

She also carried on her efforts on behalf of India, and she used the money left in the Nightingale Fund to educate midwives. Her most important work was behind her, though, and her influence was fading. To new generations of Britons, she was a revered figure from an earlier time.

With later life stretching before her, Florence returned to the scenes and people of her youth. In 1866 she went to Embley after being away for eight years, and in 1868 she spent three months with her parents at Lea Hurst. How they had aged! She noticed with sadness that her mother was growing forgetful and confused. Seeing that her parents needed her help, Florence tried to let go of old grievances. "My people never made any sacrifice for me at all. When the world said it was right for me to stay at home, I was to stay at home — when the world applauded my going to the Crimea, I was to go to the Crimea. I don't suppose any one of them ever gave five minutes thought as to which *was* right," she wrote to Clarkey. But she assured her friend, "I don't let these things 'corrode' into me now." From then on, she spent a few months with her parents every year. She also visited Parthe and Sir Harry at their London home. As Lady Verney, Parthenope had found success and fulfillment as a writer. She had published magazine articles and novels and was composing a history of the Verney family.

On January 5, 1874, Florence was not with her parents but at her own home, on South Street. That morning, at Embley, her father came down to breakfast only to realize he had forgotten his watch. He went back upstairs to get it, and while doing this small errand, he fell over and died on the spot. He was seventy-nine years old. "He always wished to go out of the world quietly — it was part of his single-minded character to do so," Florence wrote to Parthenope. "For us it is sad and dreary to have no last word or farewell, but he would have had it just so, if he could, I believe." Her illness kept Florence from attending her father's funeral.

Upon his death, the possibility that had long worried Mr. and Mrs. Nightingale finally came to pass. Mad Peter Nightingale had decreed that if William Nightingale were to die without a male heir, the estate would go to William's sister, and this was exactly what happened. Mai and Sam Smith now owned Lea Hurst, Embley, and all Mr. Nightingale's wealth. One of the first things Mai Smith did was inform the Nightingale sisters that Fanny had to move out. Mai and Sam would be living at Embley, she explained, and they were too old and ill themselves to care for her. For a while Florence lived with her mother at Sir Harry's mansion in the country, Claydon

House. Then Mai and Sam's son, Florence's cousin Shore Smith, generously invited Fanny to live with his family. The boy Florence had felt so fond of in her youth was now a married man with four young children. Shore also gave Florence a yearly allowance, as her father had done.

Time brought other changes. Florence's dear friends the Bracebridges died—Charles in 1872 and Selina in 1874. "He and she have been the creators of my life," Nightingale said, reflecting on the help and influence they provided when she was young. Fanny Nightingale died in February 1880; at the end of her life she

William Nightingale and his daughter Parthenope, Lady Verney, pose at Embley around 1870, a few years before his death.

no longer recognized her daughters. Neither Florence nor Parthe, who had painful arthritis, was present at her funeral. In 1883, Clarkey died in Paris at age ninety. And in 1885, Florence's old suitor, Richard Monckton Milnes, died while traveling in France.

For Florence Nightingale, life went on. Her chronic pain eased in the 1880s, allowing her to appear in public more often. In January 1882 she visited the Nightingale School of Nursing for the first time and toured a hospital ward. The superintendent,

Sarah Wardroper, wrote in thanks: "No words of mine can ever express the delight it gave us to welcome you, our dearly loved Chief."

Another day, she went to a London railroad station with Sir Harry Verney to welcome British soldiers arriving home from Egypt. Britain was fighting an uprising in Egypt and Sudan that threatened its access to the Suez Canal. The canal linked the Mediterranean and Red Seas and shortened the voyage from Britain to India by four thousand miles and two months. Before the canal opened in 1869, European vessels bound for India had sailed all the way around the southern tip of Africa. Nightingale felt proud of the men, though they looked "like shabby skeletons, or at least half their former size—in worn but well-cleaned campaigning uniform," she said. "A more deeply felt and less showy scene could not have been imagined."

A few days later, at a royal review of returning forces, Queen Victoria spotted a familiar figure seated between the prime minister and his wife. "I recognized Florence Nightingale, whom I had not seen for years," the queen wrote in her diary. Victoria sent a note to the famous nurse, telling her that she looked well.

Florence took rail excursions to Claydon House, where she admired the remodeling that Parthe was overseeing. Parthe and Sir Harry gave Florence her own bedroom and sitting room in the mansion, and once a year they entertained nurses from the Nightingale School. Florence always brought her cats. She made a big fuss in 1885 when a kitten named Quiz jumped out the window of a London-bound train and dashed out of sight. Nightingale soon had stationmasters up and down the line hunting for the tiny cat. One of the men discovered Quiz alive and unhurt, and the next morning he returned the mischievous runaway to its grateful mistress.

The new, more visible Florence Nightingale invited probationers into her home for tea and chats. Greeting them from her sofa and wearing a dark silk dress, she felt like "an old black beetle," she said. Many of the women stayed in touch with Nightingale after they finished their training and embarked on their careers. They felt reassured to know that they could turn to her for advice. Nightingale watched with pride as graduates of the training program took positions of responsibility. One, Rachel Williams, became the matron at St. Mary's Hospital in London. Another, Angelique Pringle, replaced Sarah Wardroper at St. Thomas's when the older woman retired.

Florence Nightingale poses among probationers enjoying an excursion to Claydon House. Behind her are Sarah Wardroper and Sir Harry Verney.

In 1887, the year she turned sixty-seven, Nightingale marked the fiftieth anniversary of her first call from God. In the same year, Queen Victoria celebrated her golden jubilee—her fiftieth year on England's throne. To honor their queen, the women of England raised a jubilee fund of seventy thousand pounds to be used for some good purpose. Following Nightingale's example, Victoria announced that the money would pay for a new school to train nurses to care for and educate the poor. It was to be called the Queen Victoria Jubilee Institute for Nurses. Nightingale disapproved of the uniform the queen designed for her probationers because it included a pendant, an unnecessary flourish.

The Jubilee Institute was one of several nursing schools that had opened in London. Schools had also been established in North America and Australia and on the European continent, many modeled on the Nightingale School. Nursing had become a respected profession for women.

The world needed nurses to staff its hospitals and workhouse infirmaries. But someday, Nightingale believed, those institutions would close their doors for good. In that far-off time, people everywhere would have learned to take care of their health. They would have done away with poverty. Why think too much about the future, though? Nightingale preferred to apply her mind to the problems of her own time. "It is no use to talk about the year 2,000," she said.

On May 12, 1890, Florence Nightingale's seventieth birthday, Parthenope died of cancer. The sisters had overcome the differences of their youth to have a close relationship in old age. Sir Harry could truthfully say to Florence, "You contributed more than anyone to what enjoyment of life was hers." Until Sir Harry died in 1894, Florence was often with him at Claydon House. She applied the organizational skills she had honed at Scutari to help him run the estate.

Benjamin Jowett also died in 1894. With the death of her cousin Shore later that year, Florence Nightingale had outlived everyone who had once been close to her. Shore's heirs sold Embley and found a tenant for Lea Hurst. They desired a simpler, more modern way of life. Within a few years, they and others would be traveling along roads in motorcars and lighting their homes with electricity. British women, craving more than home and family, would be campaigning for the right to vote.

When Queen Victoria died, on January 22, 1901, her oldest son

An aged Florence Nightingale was photographed in bed, where she spent much of her time.

took the throne, becoming King Edward VII; the Victorian era gave way to the Edwardian age. By this time Florence Nightingale had spells of memory loss, and her eyesight was failing. She relied on friendly visitors to read to her, and she dictated anything she wanted to have written down. She seldom went out anymore. In 1907, when the king bestowed on her the Order of Merit, which recognizes great achievement in learning and the arts, Shore's son Louis accepted the honor in her place. Louis stood in for her again in 1908, when she was given the Freedom of the City of London. Since medieval times, this award has recognized outstanding people who have lived or worked in the city.

At noon on August 13, 1910, ninety-year-old Florence Nightingale dozed off while sitting in her chair. Two and a half hours later, her heart was still.

Newspapers near and far announced her death and looked back on her remarkable life. They reminded readers of the frightful conditions she had found when she reached Scutari and how she "carried through under the terrible pressure of a constant race with death." The papers recalled the staggering death rate in the army hospitals before Nightingale took charge. "Without her," claimed London's *Guardian*, "our generals would soon have been left without a single man." Her wartime work made her "the heroine of the hour," stated the *New York Times*, glancing back to the days when minstrels sang about Nightingale in London's streets. The papers listed her postwar activities, which were all accomplished despite ill health: the Nightingale School, her books and pamphlets and reports, and her advice to national leaders, to name a few. Commented the *New York Times*, "Perhaps the greatest good that has resulted from her noble life has been the setting in motion of a force which has led thousands of women to devote themselves to systematic care of the sick and wounded."

Florence Nightingale had hoped to disappear from the world unnoticed, much as she had slipped into England after the Crimean War. Honoring this wish became impossible, because so many people wanted to show their respect for her. Through her steady, efficient work, Nightingale had influenced countless lives.

Thousands of mourners gathered in London on August 20. Government officials and hospital administrators filed into St. Paul's Cathedral along with nurses, soldiers in uniform, aged veterans of the Crimean War, and representatives of the royal

Horses pull the hearse bearing Florence Nightingale's coffin toward the gravesite near Embley. Three spectators stand at the side of the road. The gentlemen have removed their hats in a customary sign of respect.

family. Probationers from the Nightingale School arrived in a double-decker bus. The descendants of Shore Smith attended, as did a few Bonham Carters and Sir Harry Verney's grown children.

After the grand memorial service, a train carried Nightingale's casket to Hampshire, where another crowd had assembled. Wreaths of flowers filled the church-yard near Embley. They were from people in England and abroad—from Britain's Queen Alexandra, the widow of Edward VII, who had died in May; from nurses in Copenhagen and Tasmania, Australia; from the American Federation of Nurses; from men who had survived the charge of the Light Brigade. A seven-year-old girl named Stella Forster sent a wreath of heather she had picked herself.

Drizzle turned to a steady rain as Florence Nightingale was buried alongside her parents. The gravestone bore a simple epitaph: *F. N. Born 12 May 1820. Died 13*

August 1910. The dates marked the beginning and end of a courageous life. By going against tradition and by doing the work she saw as her duty to perform, Nightingale opened doors for women. She brought better health to many people. Beloved in life, she became a legend in death.

To Nightingale, dying was a transition, much like being born. "A human being does *not* cease to exist at death," she believed. "It is change, not destruction, which takes place."

This picture of Florence Nightingale at Scutari, based on a painting by artist
Henrietta Rae, adorned a Christmas card in 1891.

Notes

Prologue: The Night Gallery

1 "War's work": Osborne, *Scutari and Its Hospitals*, 9.

   "a face not easily forgotten": Ibid., 25.

2 "That this is the Kingdom": Goldie, *Florence Nightingale: Letters from the Crimea*, 36.

4 "She always talks": Bostridge, *Florence Nightingale*, 325.

   "Why have women passion": Nightingale, *Cassandra and Other Selections*, 205.

6 "the world is put back": Nightingale, *Collected Works*, vol. 8, 137.

   "constant progress": Cook, *The Life of Florence Nightingale*, vol. 2, 263.

1. "Mistress of All She Attempts"

8 "Books, Books, Books": Bostridge, *Florence Nightingale*, 44.

9 "The whole place": Jewitt, *Black's Tourist's Guide to Derbyshire*, 226.

11 "a shrewd little creature": Bostridge, *Florence Nightingale*, 35–36.

   "Parthe and I are so different": Ibid., 36.

   "enquiring into the why & wherefore": Ibid., 34.

   "doing arms": Gill, *Nightingales*, 95.

14 "gone mad for the want": Nightingale, *Collected Works*, vol. 1, 232.

   "She's got an oddness": Bostridge, *Florence Nightingale*, 30.

   "as precious to me": Ibid.

   "at once the happiest": O'Malley, *Florence Nightingale, 1820–1856*, 16.

   "our Baby": Ibid., 35.

   "the son of my heart": Cook, *The Life of Florence Nightingale*, vol. 1, 30.

15 "Her thirteen dolls": Gill, *Nightingales*, 100.

   "The first idea I can recollect": Nightingale, *Collected Works*, vol. 1, 90.

   "the happiest time of my life": Ibid.

15 "Conscience is a faithful": O'Malley, *Florence Nightingale, 1820–1856*, 22.

"the spirit of obedience": Cook, *The Life of Florence Nightingale*, vol. 1, 11.

"She did not understand": Nightingale, *Collected Works*, vol. 1, 90.

18 "Order & beauty": Bostridge, *Florence Nightingale*, 41.

19 "I have killed no patients": Ibid., 51.

"the passing fancy": Nightingale, *Collected Works*, vol. 1, 129.

2. A Woman with Work to Do

23 "We have some of us been rather cross": Bostridge, *Florence Nightingale*, 59.

"music-mad": Cromwell, *Florence Nightingale, Feminist*, 30.

"so beautiful, so affecting": Nightingale, *Collected Works*, vol. 7, 14.

24 "like May breezes": Bostridge, *Florence Nightingale*, 65.

"not more worshipped": Nightingale, *Collected Works*, vol. 7, 34.

25 "from morning till night": Bostridge, *Florence Nightingale*, 66.

26 "The Queen looked flushed": Ibid.

27 "one unlucky piano": Ibid., 67.

29 "to and fro upon the earth": Nightingale, *Collected Works*, vol. 1, 289.

"The house does not strike us": Ibid., 290.

"the admiration": Ibid., 291.

"The garden room" and "the yellow room": Ibid., 292.

"The green is cheerful": Ibid., 291.

"the cupboards under them": Ibid., 291.

30 "If Flo were my own daughter": Bostridge, *Florence Nightingale*, 70.

"thou, in whom we love alike to trace": Sotheby, *Lines Suggested*, 18.

32 "doing some little good": Nightingale, *Collected Works*, vol. 1, 115.

"a most awful man": Bostridge, *Florence Nightingale*, 71.

33 "And, like everything": Cook, *Life of Florence Nightingale*, vol. 1, 13.

"the very great love": Bostridge, *Florence Nightingale*, 73.

"If I am not mistaken": Ibid.

"We all liked him": O'Malley, *Florence Nightingale, 1820–1856*, 84.

34 "a work of God": Bostridge, *Florence Nightingale*, 74.

"Ladies' work has always to be fitted in": Woodham-Smith, *Florence Nightingale*, 40.

3. "Dust and Nothing"

35 "We found a fine mansion": Howe, "Reminiscences," 233.

"Go forward, if you have a vocation": Richards, *Letters and Journals of Samuel Gridley Howe*, 165.

36 "if he had been engaged": Culpepper, *Trials and Triumph*, 316.

37 "Forgive me, O God": Nightingale, *Collected Works*, vol. 2, 366.

"I shall never do anything": Cook, *The Life of Florence Nightingale*, vol. 1, 45.

38 "poor little hope": Bostridge, *Florence Nightingale*, 92.

"there would not be the same objections": Nightingale, *Collected Works*, vol. 7, 219.

39 "never leaves her": Cook, *The Life of Florence Nightingale*, vol. 1, 59.

"The other side remains": Ibid.

"Filth and poverty": Chadwick, *Report*, 10.

40 "We know her": "Julia Ward Howe Correspondence."

41 "slow circulation": Bostridge, *Florence Nightingale*, 108.

"Yes, dear": Cook, *The Life of Florence Nightingale*, vol. 1, 70.

"God Himself is at a distance": Nightingale, *Collected Works*, vol. 8, 528.

42 "more than a mother": Cook, *The Life of Florence Nightingale*, vol. 2, 236.

"in unison with her age": Nightingale, Collected Works, vol. I, 98.

43 "Looking up into that heaven": Cook, *The Life of Florence Nightingale*, vol. 1, 71.

44 "I think you would be *content*": Nightingale, *Collected Works*, vol. 7, 101.

"the stench dreadful": Ibid., 218.

45 "But still no gardens": Ibid.

46 "What does it matter": Calabria, *Florence Nightingale in Egypt and Greece*, 44.

"He calls you": Ibid.

"a warm bath": Nightingale, *Collected Works*, vol. 1, 230.

"I could not satisfy this nature": Cook, *The Life of Florence Nightingale*, vol. 1, 100.

4. The Prison Called Family

48 "your letter of this morning": Bostridge, *Florence Nightingale*, 130.

49 "a thousand times": Ibid., 131.

50 "There are only nineteen": Nightingale, *Letters from Egypt*, 24.

"Today I saw there a little orphan": Ibid.

50 "hideous": Steegmuller, *Flaubert in Egypt*, 35.

51 "Dreadful fights": Calabria, *Florence Nightingale in Egypt and Greece*, 25.

"row with Trout": Ibid., 35.

"a sort of torpor": Nightingale, *Collected Works*, vol. 4, 182.

52 "God called me": Calabria, *Florence Nightingale in Egypt and Greece*, 43.

"a country which, like its own old Nile": Nightingale, *Collected Works*, vol. 4, 439.

"the latticed windows": Nightingale, *Letters from Egypt*, 39.

"beautiful, beautiful": Ibid., 37.

"like a great sea": Ibid., 48.

"much good in the Mahometan religion": Ibid., 28.

53 "a cork model": Nightingale, *Collected Works*, vol. 7, 377.

"physically & morally ill": Bostridge, *Florence Nightingale*, 140.

54 "Christ began his mission": Calabria, *Florence Nightingale in Egypt and Greece*, 60.

55 "as if nothing could ever vex me": Ibid., 81.

"very first times": "Women and Their Work," 11.

"We say to ourselves": Ibid., 13.

56 "If an armchair": Verney, *Florence Nightingale's Pet Owl*, 18–19.

"To have knocked down": Ibid., 21.

"a bark when she was naughty": Ibid., 22–23.

58 "I can hardly open my mouth": Vicinus and Nergaard, *Ever Yours*, 45.

"My selfishness tells me": Bostridge, *Florence Nightingale*, 149.

59 "God's will": Nightingale, *Collected Works*, vol. 8, 748.

"Her path is a hard one": Gill, *Nightingales*, 263.

"he would hardly speak": Bostridge, *Florence Nightingale*, 127.

"I feel myself perishing": Ibid., 151.

"People seem to understand": Gill, *Nightingales*, 254–55.

60 "the prison which is called a family": Nightingale, *Cassandra and Other Selections*, 119.

"the laurels were in full bloom": Blackwell, *Pioneering Work*, 184.

"Do you know what I always think": Ibid., 185.

61 "medicine does not cure": Nightingale, *Collected Works*, vol. 6, 510.

5. Shadows in a Thirsty Land

62 "Young ladies of a standing in society": Bostridge, *Florence Nightingale*, 147.

63 "some great absorption": Ibid., 158.

"in order that the water": *Album of the Watering Place of Carlsbad*, unnumbered page.

64 "Everything that I have to do": Dossey, *Florence Nightingale*, 74.

"Why, oh my God": Ibid., 71.

"When he was gone": Nightingale, *Collected Works*, vol. 7, 537.

"Taking up of the arteries": Dossey, *Florence Nightingale*, 77.

"One of us": Ibid., 76.

65 "She has to consider": Ibid., 78.

66 "You yourself cannot have been more thankful": Bostridge, *Florence Nightingale*, 159.

67 "My earnest affection": Nightingale, *Collected Works*, vol. 1, 309.

"a little, strange, scrubby, boorish-looking man": Ibid., vol. 6, 515.

"Papa says capital mutton": Dossey, *Florence Nightingale*, 79.

"no grievances": Ibid.

68 "freedom and simplicity": Haight, *The George Eliot Letters*, 39.

"I was much pleased": Ibid., 45.

"nervous, fanciful, and unstable": Woodham-Smith, *Florence Nightingale*, 66.

69 "about as unspiritual": Nightingale, *Collected Works*, vol. 7, 714.

"She has a great longing": Bostridge, *Florence Nightingale*, 175.

"The flood whirls": Ibid.

"absolutely no disease": Ibid.

"Sir James says": Nightingale, *Collected Works*, vol. 1, 132.

70 "a stranded ship": Ibid., vol. 3, 266.

"has little or none": Vicinus and Nergaard, *Ever Yours*, 56.

71 "Flo you know has more": Bostridge, *Florence Nightingale*, 181.

"these ideas, so busy working": Ibid., 182.

"for having a child": Ibid.

"an old actress": Nightingale, *Collected Works*, vol. 7, 724.

72 "The first snowdrops": Ibid., vol. 1, 417.

"She bears it": Ibid., 420.

72 "I hope the sun shines": Ibid., 422.

"great had been the occasion": Gill, *Nightingales*, 281.

"till the last of her moments": Gill, *Nightingales*, 281.

"I shall want her company": Bostridge, *Florence Nightingale*, 184.

73 "prevented by their position": Low, *The Charities of London* (London: Sampson Law, 1850), 50.

74 "by a representative system": Cook, *The Life of Florence Nightingale*, vol. 1, 138.

"Parthe can no more control": Bostridge, *Florence Nightingale*, 185.

6. "But One Person in England"

75 "I look upon your position": Nightingale, *Collected Works*, vol. 8, 23.

77 "changed one housemaid": Ibid., vol. 12, 110.

79 "You foolish child": Bostridge, *Florence Nightingale*, 193.

"We well know that the great work": Nightingale, *Collected Works*, vol. 12, 97.

80 "to the vast abyss": Roe, "To W. T. Harris, Esq.," 512.

"How is the cholera generated": "History of the Origin, Progress and Mortality of the Cholera Morbus," 557.

81 "microscopic insects": Ibid., 558.

"The poison may be wafted": Roe, "To W. T. Harris, Esq.," 512.

"fresh air in the place of the deadly poison": Ibid.

"The prostitutes come in perpetually": Haldane, *Mrs. Gaskell and Her Friends*, 93.

82 "Take the handle off": Dossey, *Florence Nightingale*, 98.

83 "tall; very slight": Haldane, *Mrs. Gaskell and Her Friends*, 98–99.

"must be a creature": Ibid., 100–01.

"sense of existence": Ibid., 91.

85 "The beef being very like coarse mahogany": Fleming and Hamilton, *The Crimean War*, xii.

"the wretched beggar": Ibid., xiii.

"Not only are there not sufficient surgeons": Untitled report from Constantinople in the *London Times*, October 12, 1854.

86 "Why have we no Sisters of Charity?": "Hospital Assistants in the East," *London Times*, October 14, 1854.

87 "I receive numbers of offers": Goldie, *Florence Nightingale: Letters from the Crimea*, 23–24.

87 "None of her previous life": Cook, *The Life of Florence Nightingale*, vol. 1, 155.

"Superintendent of the female nursing establishment": Goldie, *Florence Nightingale: Letters from the Crimea*, 26.

88 "Miss Nightingale": Herbert, "Nurses for the Wounded."

"God speed you": Cook, *The Life of Florence Nightingale*, vol. 1, 161.

89 "I hear you are going": Ibid.

"Poor little beastie": Verney, *Florence Nightingale's Pet Owl*, 36.

7. The Horrors

90 "It was like a huge slaughter-house": "A Volunteer with Florence Nightingale," 415–16.

"vast field of suffering": Osborne, *Scutari and Its Hospitals*, 12.

"I had passed weeks": Ibid., 8–9.

"a condition disgusting to see": Ibid., 19.

91 "inexpressibly shocked": Ibid., 8.

"the largest, the most beautiful": Stafford, *History of the War in Russia and Turkey*, 287.

"the world wondered": Widmer, "Grandfather and Florence Nightingale," 569.

93 "Occasionally the roof is torn off": Goldie, *Florence Nightingale: Letters from the Crimea*, 37.

94 "a wee room": Bostridge, *Florence Nightingale*, 224.

"the Bird": Cook, *The Life of Florence Nightingale*, vol. 1, 182.

"to hear a man bawl": Syme, "Professor Syme on Chloroform in Operations," *London Times*, October 12, 1854.

"We tried to console ourselves": Richardson, *Nurse Sarah Anne*, 83.

95 "If I'd known": Goldie, *Florence Nightingale: Letters from the Crimea*, 36.

"She has one flannel petticoat": Bostridge, *Florence Nightingale*, 233.

"400 wounded arriving": Goldie, *Florence Nightingale: Letters from the Crimea*, 33.

96 "from thirty iron-mouths": *The Battles of the Crimea* (New York: O. F. Parsons, 1855), 73.

97 "seemed encircled by fire": Ibid., 81.

"the boldest struggle ever witnessed": Ibid., 83.

"There was neither basin, towel nor soap": Nightingale, *Collected Works*, vol. 14, 68.

98 "For when one poor fellow": Ibid., 64.

"that they could not take it off": Bostridge, *Florence Nightingale*, 515.

"Flo has in this week": Nightingale, *Collected Works*, vol. 14, 65.

98 "the deathbeds": Ibid., 66.

100 "I am really cook": Goldie, *Florence Nightingale: Letters from the Crimea*, 79.

"for these miserable Hospitals": Ibid., 81.

"We have not seen a drop": "The Hospitals at Scutari."

"rather high of stature": Soyer, *Soyer's Culinary Campaign*, 153–54.

101 "mind was quite overpowered": Brandon, *The People's Chef*, 239.

102 "exert all that science can do": Nightingale, *Collected Works*, vol. 14, 131.

"marks of much" and "The wind blew": *Professional Papers of the Corps of Royal Engineers*, vol. 24 (Chatham, UK: MacKay, 1898), 38.

103 "*We* pulled this Hospital": Goldie, *Florence Nightingale: Letters from the Crimea*, 134–35.

104 "Her nerve is wonderful": Osborne, *Scutari and Its Hospitals*, 26.

8. An Angel with a Lamp

105 "She is a 'ministering angel'": "Florence Nightingale," *Ladies' Repository*, 1858, 361.

"In conversation": Soyer, *Soyer's Culinary Campaign*, 154.

106 "her every word and action": Osborne, *Scutari and Its Hospitals*, 26.

"There is not one": "Who Is 'Mrs' Nightingale?" *Examiner*, October 28, 1854.

107 "the mother of so heroic a woman": Bostridge, *Florence Nightingale*, 258.

"fine fellows" and "It was most touching": Ibid.

"not like celebrity": Ibid.

"What next?": Ibid., 259.

108 "she's here, there, and everywhere": "Narrative of Foreign Events," 17.

"The immense amount of writing": Bostridge, *Florence Nightingale*, 259.

"Good public": Nightingale, *Collected Works*, vol. 5, 232.

"came upon the long wards": Seacole, *Wonderful Adventures*, 91–92.

109 "Many of them had that strange": Ibid., 94.

110 "You have sacrificed the cause": Nightingale, *Collected Works*, vol. 14, 83.

113 "I took it as a full reward": Goldie, *Florence Nightingale: Letters from the Crimea*, 130.

"This is the most flowery place": Ibid.

"with a bullet in his eye": Ibid., 131.

115 "as bad an attack": Dossey, *Florence Nightingale*, 162.

116 "Her qualities of soul": Verney, *Florence Nightingale's Pet Owl*, 32.

116 "I cannot tell you": Goldie, *Florence Nightingale: Letters from the Crimea*, 133.

117 "looks pretty well": Bostridge, *Florence Nightingale*, 281.

"Give them books": Nightingale, *Collected Works*, vol. 14, 342.

118 "Mother Brickbat": Ibid., 259.

"At first I thought": Hornby, *In and Around Stamboul*, vol. 1, 185.

"Her face is long": Ibid., 186

119 "the rightful position": Goldie, *Florence Nightingale: Letters from the Crimea*, 215.

"Would not you like to see": Ibid., 260.

9. Nightingale Power

120 "The last of our Invalids": Goldie, *Florence Nightingale: Letters from the Crimea*, 281.

"I have been": Nightingale, *Collected Works*, vol. 14, 472.

"I see her at times": Bostridge, *Florence Nightingale*, 297.

121 "like a bird": Bostridge, *Florence Nightingale*, 305.

"a blessing": Ibid.

"A little tinkle": Cook, *The Life of Florence Nightingale*, vol. 1, 304.

"& I cannot believe": Dossey, *Florence Nightingale*, 182.

123 "living skeletons": Goldie, *Florence Nightingale: Letters from the Crimea*, 222.

"I stand at the Altar": Ibid., 296.

125 "The effect is not very pretty": James, *Rosebery*, 66.

"a rather cold, stiff, reserved person": Nightingale, *Collected Works*, vol. 5, 413–14.

"like a person who wanted": Ibid., 415.

127 "For the next three or four months": Goldie, *Florence Nightingale: Letters from the Crimea*, 286.

"Little War Office": Nightingale, *Collected Works*, vol. 14, 1049.

"the Nightingale power": Cook, *The Life of Florence Nightingale*, vol. 1, 214.

"There was nothing different": Vicinus and Nergaard, *Ever Yours*, 177.

128 "so entirely forgets herself": Bostridge, *Florence Nightingale*, 322.

"Our soldiers enlist": Nies and McEwen, *Community Health Nursing*, 31.

130 "Nobody who has not worked with her": Cromwell, *Florence Nightingale, Feminist*, 185.

132 "I fear Florence's power of work": Bostridge, *Florence Nightingale*, 326.

133 "He woos her like a soldier": Ibid., 347.

133 "God bless you": Ibid., 350.

134 "It is beautiful only": Clough, *The Poems of Arthur Hugh Clough*, 170.

10. Maid of All Work

136 "sober, honest, truthful": House of Commons, *Accounts and Papers*, vol. 22, 78.

139 "poison the blood": Nightingale, *Notes on Hospitals*, 7.

"are very often not symptoms": Nightingale, *Notes on Nursing*, 8.

"The very walls": Ibid., 60.

"I have met": Ibid., 26.

140 "His scheme for us": Nightingale, *Cassandra and Other Selections*, 59.

"no food for our heads": Ibid., 220.

"Awake, ye women": Ibid., 229.

141 "You know I don't believe": Cook, *The Life of Florence Nightingale*, vol. 1, 401.

"sleep, fresh air, regular food": Dossey, *Florence Nightingale,* 245.

142 "Poor Florence": Ibid.

"Grief fills up the room": Ibid.

"I am his real widow": Vicinus and Nergaard, *Ever Yours*, 232.

"angelic temper": Cromwell, *Florence Nightingale, Feminist*, 211.

"He constantly kept": Nightingale, *Army Sanitary Administration*, 10–11.

"all the money-making": Bostridge, *Florence Nightingale*, 382.

"Oh Jonathan": Cromwell, *Florence Nightingale, Feminist*, 212.

143 "truly a beautiful house": Bostridge, *Florence Nightingale*, 409.

"The golden bowl": Woodham-Smith, *Florence Nightingale*, 437.

"Little time is lost": Tollemache, *Benjamin Jowett*, 1.

"cherubic chirp": Ibid., 2.

144 "at times clouds your mind": Quinn and Prest, *Dear Miss Nightingale*, 49.

145 "Florence the First": Vicinus and Nergaard, *Ever Yours*, 300.

"Maid of all (dirty) work": Ibid.

147 "From that moment": Nightingale, *Collected Works*, vol. 6, 329.

"Great care and attention": House of Commons, *Accounts and Papers*, vol. 22, 377.

148 "in most of these wards": Ibid.

II. A Noble Life

150 "the germs of various low forms": Lister, "On a New Method," 327.

"Where are these little beasts": Porter, *The Greatest Benefit to Mankind*, 372.

152 "The principal feature": "St. Thomas's Hospital," *Lancet*, October 22, 1870, 578.

"to have high principles": Nightingale, *Florence Nightingale to Her Nurses*, 90.

"My people never made any sacrifice": Lesser, *Clarkey*, 183.

153 "He always wished": Nightingale, *Collected Works*, vol. 1, 273.

154 "He and she have been the creators": Shepherd, *The Crimean Doctors*, vol. 2, 523.

155 "No words of mine": Cook, *The Life of Florence Nightingale*, vol. 2, 327.

"like shabby skeletons": Ibid., 335–36.

"I recognized Florence Nightingale": Nightingale, *Collected Works*, vol. 5, 422.

156 "an old black beetle": Bostridge, *Florence Nightingale*, 457–58.

157 "It is no use": Ibid., 507.

"You contributed more": Woodham-Smith, *Florence Nightingale*, 581–82.

159 "carried through": "Death of Miss Florence Nightingale," *Guardian*, August 15, 1910.

"Without her": Ibid.

"the heroine of the hour": "Miss Nightingale Dies, Aged Ninety," *New York Times*, August, 15, 1910.

"Perhaps the greatest good": Ibid.

161 "A human being does *not* cease": Calabria and Macrae, *Suggestions for Thought*, 148.

Back cover: "A hundred struggle and drown": Nightingale, *Cassandra and Other Selections*, 208.

SELECTED BIBLIOGRAPHY

Album of the Watering Place of Carlsbad. Siegburg, Germany: German Photogravure Co., 1900.

Blackwell, Elizabeth. *Pioneering Work in Opening the Medical Profession to Women.* London: Longmans, Green, and Company, 1895.

Bostridge, Mark. *Florence Nightingale: The Woman and Her Legend.* London: Penguin, 2008.

Brandon, Ruth. *The People's Chef.* New York: Walker and Company, 2004.

Calabria, Michael D. *Florence Nightingale in Egypt and Greece: Her Diary and "Visions."* Albany: State University of New York Press, 1997.

Calabria, Michael D., and Janet A. Macrae, eds. *Suggestions for Thought: Selections and Commentaries.* Philadelphia: University of Pennsylvania Press, 1994.

Chadwick, Edwin. *Report . . . on an Inquiry into the Sanitary Condition of the Labouring Population of Great Britain.* London: W. Clowes and Sons, 1842.

Clough, Arthur Hugh. *The Poems of Arthur Hugh Clough.* Oxford, UK: Clarendon Press, 1951.

Cook, Edward. *The Life of Florence Nightingale.* 2 vols. London: Macmillan and Co., 1914.

Cromwell, Judith Lissauer. *Florence Nightingale, Feminist.* Jefferson, NC: McFarland and Co., 2013.

Culpepper, Marilyn Mayer. *Trials and Triumph.* East Lansing: Michigan State University Press, 1991.

Dossey, Barbara Montgomery. *Florence Nightingale.* Springhouse, PA: Springhouse, 2000.

Fleming, Angela Michelli, and John Maxwell Hamilton, eds. *The Crimean War as Seen by Those Who Reported It.* Baton Rouge: Louisiana State University Press, 2009.

"Florence Nightingale." *Ladies' Repository,* 1858, 358–64.

Gill, Gillian. *Nightingales.* New York: Random House, 2005.

Goldie, Sue M., ed. *Florence Nightingale: Letters from the Crimea.* Manchester, UK: Mandolin, 1997.

Haight, Gordon S., ed. *The George Eliot Letters.* Vol. 2. London: Geoffrey Cumberlege, 1954.

Haldane, Elizabeth. *Mrs. Gaskell and Her Friends.* Freeport, NY: Books for Libraries Press, 1970.

Herbert, Sidney. "Nurses for the Wounded." *London Morning Chronicle,* October 24, 1854.

"History of the Origin, Progress and Mortality of the Cholera Morbus." *London Medical Gazette, or Journal of Practical Medicine* (1849): 507–11, 556–59, 600–602.

Hornby, Mrs. Edmund. *In and Around Stamboul.* Vol. 1. London: Richard Bentley, 1858.

House of Commons. *Accounts and Papers of the House of Commons, 1867–68.* Vol. 22. London: Parliament, House of Commons, 1868.

Howe, Julia Ward. "Reminiscences of Julia Ward Howe." *Atlantic Monthly,* February 1899, 219–35.

James, Robert Rhodes. *Rosebery.* London: Weidenfeld and Nicolson, 1963.

Jewitt, Llewellyn, ed. *Black's Tourist's Guide to Derbyshire: Its Towns, Watering Places, Dales, and Mansions.* Edinburgh: Adam and Charles Black, 1868.

"Julia Ward Howe Correspondence." Perkins School for the Blind Archive.

Lesser, Margaret, ed. *Clarkey: A Portrait in Letters of Mary Clarke Mohl.* Oxford: Oxford University Press, 1984.

Lister, Joseph. "On a New Method of Treating Compound Fracture, Abscess, Etc." *Lancet* (March 16, 1867): 326–29.

Luddy, Maria, ed. *The Crimean Journals of the Sisters of Mercy.* Dublin: Four Courts Press, 2004.

"Narrative of Foreign Events." *Household Narrative of Current Events* (December 27, 1854–January 27, 1855): 11–23.

Nies, Mary A., and Melanie McEwen. *Community Health Nursing.* Philadelphia: Saunders, 2001.

Nightingale, Florence. *Army Sanitary Administration and Its Reform.* London: McCorquodale and Co., 1862.

———. *Cassandra and Other Selections from Suggestions for Thought.* London: Pickering and Chatto, 1991.

———. *The Collected Works of Florence Nightingale.* Edited by Lynn McDonald and Gérard Vallée. 16 vols. Ontario, Canada: Wilfrid Laurier University Press, 2002–12.

———. *Florence Nightingale to Her Nurses.* London: Macmillan and Company, 1914.

———. *Letters from Egypt: A Journey on the Nile, 1849–1850.* New York: Weidenfeld and Nicolson, 1987.

———. *Notes on Hospitals.* London: John W. Parker and Son, 1859.

———. *Notes on Nursing: What It Is, and What It Is Not.* New York: D. Appleton and Co., 1860.

O'Malley, Ida B. *Florence Nightingale, 1820–1856.* London: Thornton Butterworth, 1931.

Osborne, Sydney Godolphin. *Scutari and Its Hospitals.* London: Dickinson Brothers, 1855.

Porter, Roy. *The Greatest Benefit to Mankind.* New York: W. W. Norton and Co., 1997.

Quinn, Vincent, and John Prest, eds. *Dear Miss Nightingale: A Selection of Benjamin Jowett's Letters to Florence Nightingale, 1860–1893.* Oxford, UK: Clarendon Press, 1987.

Richards, Laura E., ed. *Letters and Journals of Samuel Gridley Howe.* Boston: Dana Estes and Co., 1909.

Richardson, Robert G. *Nurse Sarah Anne: With Florence Nightingale at Scutari.* London: John Murray, 1977.

Roe, Edward T. "To W. T. Harris, Esq., Chairman of the Board of Health." *London Medical Gazette, or Journal of Practical Medicine* (1849): 512–13.

Seacole, Mary. *Wonderful Adventures of Mrs. Seacole in Many Lands.* New York: Kaplan, 2009.

Shepherd, John. *The Crimean Doctors.* Liverpool, UK: Liverpool University Press, 1991.

Sotheby, William. *Lines Suggested by the Third Meeting of the British Association for the Advancement of Science, Held at Cambridge, in June, 1833.* London: G. and W. Nicol, 1834.

Soyer, Alexis. *Soyer's Culinary Campaign.* London: G. Routledge and Company, 1857.

Stafford, W. Cooke. *History of the War in Russia and Turkey.* Liverpool, UK: Peter Jackson, 1855.

Stanmore, Arthur Hamilton-Gordon. *Sidney Herbert, Lord Herbert of Lea.* Vol. 2. London: John Murray, 1906.

Steegmuller, Francis, ed. *Flaubert in Egypt: A Sensibility on Tour.* New York: Penguin, 1972.

Tollemache, Lionel A. *Benjamin Jowett: Master of Balliol.* London: Edward Arnold, 1904.

Verney, Parthenope. *Florence Nightingale's Pet Owl, Athena.* San Francisco: Grabhorn-Hoyem, 1970.

Vicinus, Martha, and Bea Nergaard, eds. *Ever Yours, Florence Nightingale: Selected Letters.* Cambridge, MA: Harvard University Press, 1990.

"A Volunteer with Florence Nightingale." *Literary Digest,* September 10, 1910, 415–16.

Widmer, Carolyn Ladd. "Grandfather and Florence Nightingale." *American Journal of Nursing* (May 1955): 569–71.

"Women and Their Work." *Ecclesiastic and Theologian* (January/December 1855): 6–27.

Woodham-Smith, Cecil. *Florence Nightingale, 1820–1910.* London: Constable, 1950.

PICTURE CREDITS

Author's collection: 5, 9, 10, 17, 19, 38, 44 (top), 44 (bottom), 55, 57, 63, 89, 133, 134, 144

Billy Rose Theatre Division, The New York Public Library for the Performing Arts, Astor, Lenox and Tilden Foundations: 40

Collection du Musée de Boulogne-sur-Mer, © Philippe Beurtheret: 21

Fliedner Kulturstiftung Kaiserswerth: 65, 66

Florence Nightingale Museum, London, UK / Bridgeman Images: 28, 32, 76, 107, 117, 121, 122, 138, 154

Hampshire Record Office: 94M72/F613/8: 13

Hampshire Record Office: 94M72/F614/4: 106

Hampshire Record Office: 97M81/23/23: 160

Library of Congress: 3, 4, 8, 24, 31, 34, 36, 43, 49, 51, 53, 68, 91, 101, 103, 162

National Library of Medicine: 47, 61, 92, 121, 124, 131

© National Portrait Gallery, London: 22, 25, 27, 126

Picture Collection, The New York Public Library, Astor, Lenox and Tilden Foundations: 28

Private Collection / Bridgeman Images: 82, 110

Private Collection / © Look and Learn / Elgar Collection / Bridgeman Images: 78

Private Collection / © Look and Learn / Illustrated Papers Collection / Bridgeman Images: 70

Private Collection / © Look and Learn / Peter Jackson Collection / Bridgeman Images: 80

Wellcome Library, London. Wellcome Images: viii, 12, 73, 83, 84, 86, 95, 96, 99, 109, 112, 114, 115, 116, 128, 129, 146, 148, 151, 156, 158

Index

NOTES: FN = Florence Nightingale. Page numbers in **bold** indicate images/pictures

Albert of Saxe-Coburg, Prince, 107, 125, **126**, 136, 142

Amphitrite shipwreck, 20, **21**

animals, love for, 18–19, 143, 155

antiseptic methods, 150–151

Army Nurse Corps, **4**

Athena the owl, 53, 56, 89, 116, **117**

Athens, Greece, trip to, 53

Atkins, Samuel, 98

Balaclava, Battle of, 95–96, 110

Balmoral Castle, Scotland, 123–125

Barrack Hospital, Scutari
    closing at war's end, 120
    conditions, 2, 87, 90, 92, 97
    depictions of FN at, viii, **89, 92, 99, 106**
    doctors at, 93–94, 98
    FN's nursing mission to, 87–104
    food preparation, 100–101
    notes and data about, 128, 130
    nurses' living quarters, 93–94
    physical structure, size, 91
    sanitary commission at, 102–103
    supply problems, 99–100
    travel to, **3**

Bell, Currer. *See* Brontë, Charlotte

Bennett, John Hughes, 150

Blackwell, Dr. Elizabeth, 60–61, **61**, 75

Bonham Carter, Hilary, **13**, **47**, 141, 143

Bonham Carter, John and Joanna, 13

Bonham Carter, William, 40

boys, schooling given, 16

Bracebridge, Charles and Selina
    deaths, 154
    distribution of *Times* fund money, 98
    support for FN's nursing ambitions, 41–42, 54, 59, 62, 71, 72
    travels with FN, 41–43, 48, 50–51

Bridgeman, Mother Mary Francis (nursing nun), 118–119

Broad Street water pump, 82

Brontë, Charlotte (*Jane Eyre*), 39–40

Brownlow Hill Workhouse Infirmary, Liverpool, 147–148

brucellosis (Crimean fever), 115–117, 128

Burlington Hotel, London, FN's residence at, 127, 141–142

Cairo, Egypt, visit to, 50–51

Canning, Lady Charlotte, 72–74, 79

Carlsbad (Karlovy Vary, Czech Republic), spas at, 63, **63**

Catholics. *See also* nurses
    in Crimean nursing mission, 88
    FN's interest in teachings of, 45
    as patients at charity hospital, 77
    persecution, 77
cats, devotion to, 143, 155
Chapman, John, 67–68
charity hospital. *See* Establishment for
        Gentlewomen During Illness
charity schools, 16
Chatham, England, army medical college, 138
cholera
    London epidemic, 79–81
    theories explaining, 81, **82**
    treatments, **83**
    water transmission, 82
Christie, Sara, 11, 15
Clark, Charlotte, 69
Clark, James, 68–69, 123
Clarke, Elizabeth Hay, 24
Clarke, Mary (Clarkey, Madame Mohl), 24, **25**, 42,
        70–71, 141, 152–154
Clarke, Mary (housekeeper), 75, 88, 97
Clarkey. *See* Clarke, Mary
Claydon House, 153, 155–157
Clough, Arthur Hugh, 134–135, 137, 141
Clough, Blanche Smith, 134, 142
Clough, Florence, 135
cold-water cure, 67
Covent Garden, London, 79, **80**
covered wagon, **121**
Crimean fever. *See* brucellosis
Crimean War. *See also* Barrack Hospital
    army camps, 85–86, 125–126
    Battle of Balaclava, 95–96, 110
    Battle of Inkerman, 96–97, **115**
    casualties, 2, 96–97
    ending of, 119

    hospital tours, 111–114, **116**
    reporting about, 84–85
    underlying causes, 2, 84

Darwin, Charles, 26
Deaconess Institute, Kaiserswerth, 54–55, 59, 61,
        62–65, **65**, **66**
Dickens, Charles, 26, 38

Edward VII, King of England, 158, 160
Egypt
    Suez Canal defense, 155
    trip to, 48–52
Eliot, George (Mary Ann Evans), 67–68, **68**
Embley, Hampshire, (Nightingale home)
    family return to, 29
    FN's long absence from, 152
    photograph, **10**
    renovations, 25–26
    Shore Smith's inheritance of, 153, 158
Establishment for Gentlewomen During Illness,
        72–79, **76**
European tour, 20–23

Farr, Dr. William, 129, **129**, 138
Flaubert, Gustave, 50
Fliedner, Theodor, 54, **55**, 65
Florence, Italy, birth in, 7–8
Fowler, Dr. Richard, 36, 69
France, family tour of, 20–23
Freedom of the City award, 158–159

Gaskell, Elizabeth, 82–84, **84**
General Hospital, Balaclava, 113–115, 118–119
General Hospital, Scutari, 93
Geneva Medical College, 60
Genoa, Italy, 23, **24**
German Hospital, London, 61–62

germ theory of disease, 150–151

Giffard, Reverend Jervis, 18

Gillespie, Reverend, math studies with, 32

governesses, social status, 11, 15, 73

Gray, Elisabeth C. H., 107

Grillage, Peter, 122, **122**

Hall, Dr. John, 94, **95**, 114, 118

Herbert, Elizabeth (Liz), 44, **44**, 60, 88, 108, 142

Herbert, Sidney
 diabetes, kidney disease, 141–142
 friendship with FN, 44
 and nursing missions to Scutari, 85–89, 110
 portrait, **44**
 Royal Commission on the Health of the Army,
  126–131

Hôpital des Enfants Malades, Paris, 71

hospitals. *See also* Barrack Hospital; Establishment
  for Gentlewomen During Illness *and other*
  hospitals and infirmaries
 design of, 139, 151–152
 filthy conditions, 36–38, 44–45
 military, work to improve, 85, 102, 123–132,
  144–145, 159

Howe, Julia Ward, 35–36, **36**, 40

Howe, Samuel Gridley, 35–36

India, health problems for soldiers and citizens,
  144–146, **146**

Inkerman, Battle of, 96–97, **115**

The Institution of Kaiserswerth on the Rhine:
  For the Practical Training of Deaconesses
  (Nightingale), 55–56, 59

Ireland, visits to, 69

Italy, visits to, 7–8, 23, 42–44, 52

Jane Eyre (Brontë), 39–40

Johnson, Dr., cold-water cure, 67

Jones, Agnes, 147, 149

Jones, William, 122, **122**

Jowett, Benjamin, 143–145, **144**, 158

Kaiserswerth. *See* Deaconess Institute, Kaiserswerth

"Lady with the Lamp" phrase, 3, 105, **106**, **162**

La Maternité hospital, Paris, 60

Lawrence, John, 145

Lea Hurst, Derbyshire (Nightingale home), 7–9, **9**,
  69–70, 152

Lefroy, Colonel John, 118–119

The Life and Death of Athena, an Owlet from the
  Parthenon (P. Nightingale), 116, **117**

Light Brigade, charge of, 95–96, **96**

Lister, Joseph, 150–151, **151**

"Little War Office," 127–128

Lucrezia Borgia (Donizetti opera), 23

Macdonald, John, 98, 105

Maison de la Providence (Sisters of Charity hospital),
  Paris, 72

mathematics, FN's studies of, 29–30, 32–33

mentally ill, poor treatment of, 78

miasma theory of disease, 81, **82**, 97, 139

middle class, rise of, 11, 26

Middlesex Hospital, London, 81

Milnes, Richard Monckton (Lord Houghton)
 death, 154
 portrait, **34**
 support for FN's nursing expedition, 89
 wooing of FN, 33–34, 40, 46–47, 59

Mohl, Julius, 42, 71

Mohl, Mary Clarke. *See* Clarke, Mary (Clarkey,
  Madame Mohl)

newspapers
 articles about FN in, 105–106, 108, 159

articles about India in, 145

Crimean War news in, 85–86, 96–97, 100, 128

London Times fund for sick and wounded soldiers, 98

Nicholson, George and Anne, 13, 33, 59

Nicholson, Henry, 29, 58–59

Nicholson, Marianne, 27, **28**, 59

Nicholson, William, 33

Nightingale, Fanny Smith

charity work, 18

death, 154

disapproval for FN's ambitions, 25, 29–30, 36–37, 127

education of daughters, 11, 30

eviction from Embley, 153

family business, 11

home management, charity work, 7, 18

marriage and children, 7

physical appearance, personality, 8–9, 25

portrait of, **12**

religious faith, **12**

response to FN's fame, 106–107, 127–128

siblings, extended family, 13–14

social aspirations, ambitions, 8–9, 24–26, 37, 42, 47, 71

support for FN's ambitions and activities, 32, 61, 65–66, 71, 88

work on FN's behalf, 127–128

Nightingale, Florence. *See also* Barrack Hospital; Crimean War; Establishment for Gentlewomen; Nightingale School of Nursing

acceptance of germ theory and antisepsis, 151

activities on behalf of soldiers, 3–4, 117, 123, 128–129, 144–146, **146**, 155

birth and childhood, 7–9, 12–15

care for the sick and dying, 15, 18–19, 31–32, 58, 64, 72, 84, 104, 161

curiosity, love for learning, 11, 16, 29, 32–33, 45, 47, 71

death, 159

desire to work behind the scenes, 127

energy, work ethic, 1–2, 4, 121–123, 128–130

epitaph, 160–161

European tour, 20–25

fame, 3, 105–106, 121–123, 127–128

funeral and burial, 159–161

homages to following death, 159–160

illnesses, depression, exhaustion, 15, 40–41, 59, 114–115, 120–121, 132–133, 158

images showing, viii, **12**, **13**, **22**, **28**, **32**, **57**, **92**, **115**, **124**, **156**, **158**

The Institution of Kaiserswerth on the Rhine, 55–56, 59

London debut, 26

London home, 143

love and care for animals, 12, 18–19

love for music, 23

management style, 103–104, 110–111, 117–119

math studies, 33

memorial service and funeral, 159–160, **160**

Notes on Hospitals, 139

Notes on Matters Affecting the Health, Efficiency and Hospital Administration of the British Army, 130

Notes on Nursing, 139–140

nursing studies, 36–37, 40, 50, 54–55, 61, 64–65, 68–69

nursing expedition to the Crimea, 1–3, 87–104

old age, 153–156

physical appearance, 1, 25, 35, 83, 116, 118, 125

record keeping and statistics, 14, 21, **76**, 130–131, **131**

resentment of mother and sister, 11, 42, 58, 64, 67, 70, 127, 132, 152–153

response to death of friends, 141–142, 157–158

Nightingale, Florence (*ctd.*)

spiritual mission, religious calling, 19, 34–35, 37, 45–46, 67, 79, 83, 86–87, 140, 157

standards of cleanliness, 2, 42, 97, 139, 148

Suggestions for Thought, 140, 143

suitors and marriage proposals, 33

temper, anger, 36–39, 140–141

thirtieth birthday, 54

travels, 23, 41–42, 51–52

views on dying and death, 151

and women's independence, 4–6, 33–34

work on behalf of needs in India, 145–146

writings, 138–140

Nightingale, "Mad Peter," 7–8, 153

Nightingale, Parthenope (Parthe, Pop, Lady Verney)

artistic talents, 11, 21, 28, **57, 117**

assistance with FN's work, 117, 127–128

on Athena the owl, 56

birth, 7

childhood, 12

conflicts with, disapproval and resentment of FN, 11, 15, 58, 64, 66–67, 69–70, 74, 79, 83–84, 88

death, 157

disinterest in lessons, music, 11, 16, 27

European tour, 20–25

frailty, illnesses, 7, 9, 16, 25, 28–29, 52, 58, 61, 63, 68–70

images showing, **12, 22, 133, 154**

Julia Ward Howe's comments on, 35

The Life and Death of Athena, an Owlet from the Parthenon, 116, **117**

London debut, 16–17

parents' concerns about, 24, 74, 133

physical appearance, personality, 25, 35, 74, 83

response to FN's fame, 108, 121

social conformity, 16, 37, 42, 47, 58

support for FN's nursing missions, 87–88, 108

Verney's courtship and marriage to, 133–134, 153

Nightingale, William (William Shore)

avoidance of involvement in family conflicts, 26, 30, 39, 48, 58, 74, 107

banking business, 10–11

carriage design, 21

death, 153

education of daughters, 15–16, 20

eye ailment and treatment, 67

financial support for FN, 45, 71, 74, 154

inheritance, 16

marriage and family, 7–8

photograph showing, **154**

purchase of Embley, 9–10

religious faith, 12

response to FN's fame, 106–107, 127–128

support for nursing and nurses, 62

Nightingale Fund, 123, 135–136, 152

"Nightingale in the East" song, 109

"the Nightingale power," 127, 135, 145

Nightingale School of Nursing. *See also* probationers (student nurses)

acceptance of germ theory and antiseptic methods, 151

first students/course of study, 136–137

FN's role as overseer, 137, 152

FN' visit to after long absence, 154–155

as part of St. Thomas's Hospital, 136–138, **138,** 152

Verney's involvement with, 152

North and South (Gaskell), 82–83

Notes on Hospitals (Nightingale), 139

Notes on Matters Affecting the Health, Efficiency and Hospital Administration of the British Army (Nightingale), 130

Notes on Nursing (Nightingale), 139–140

nurses

drunkenness among, 38, 94

nursing nuns and sisters, 38–39, 50, 71, 95, 110, 117

obedience to doctors, 94

uniforms, 95, 136, 157

in workhouses, 146–147

nursing. *See also* Nightingale School for Nursing
and individual hospitals and infirmaries

as charitable endeavor, 54–56

at home, 139–140

Queen Victoria Jubilee Institute for Nurses, 157

school for, in Liverpool, 148–149

as a secular profession, 62

as a woman's profession, 61

Order of Merit, 158

Osborne, Reverend Sydney

descriptions of FN, 104, 106

ministry at Scutari, 90–91, 97–98

Palmerston, Lord, 86, 102, 132

Panmure, Lord, 126–127, 130–132

Paris, France, visits to, 23–24, 42, 71

Parthenope (Nile boat), 50–52

Pasteur, Louis, 150

the poor

charity work by women, 18, 55–56

hospitals and nursing for, 147, 149, 157

living conditions and illnesses, 37, 39, 82–83, 147

poor law, 39, 149

workhouses, 146–147

probationers (student nurses)

at Claydon House, **156**

clothing, 136

education given, 136–137, 151

FN's support for, 152–153, 156

meals, **138**

Queen Victoria Jubilee Institute for Nurses, 157

Rae, Henrietta, **162**

Rathbone, William, 147–149

Roe, Dr. Edward T., 81

Rome, Italy, visit to, 41, 43, 45

Roosh (dog), 122, **122**

Royal Commission on the Health of the Army, 130

Royal Naval College ball, **17**

Royal Statistical Society, FN's admission to, 131

Royal Victoria Military Hospital, Netley, FN's review
of plans for, 131–132

Sairey Gamp (Dickens character), **38**

Salisbury Infirmary, 36–37

San Gallicano Hospital, Rome, 45

San Giacomo Hospital, Rome, 44–45

sanitary commission, 102–103, 145

Santa Columba, Madre, friendship with, 45–46, 52

Scutari, Turkey. *See also* Barrack Hospital, Scutari;
Crimean War

FN's departure from, 120

travel to, 2

Turkish burial grounds, 91

Seacole, Mary, work as Crimean nurse, 108–110

Sensi, Felicetta, FN's financial support for, 45

Shore, Grandmother, death, 72

Sisters of Charity, nursing work, 50, 86, **86**

Sisters of St. John's House, London, 62

Smith, Fred, 13–14, 31–32

Smith, Jane, 31–33

Smith, Julia, 14, 31

Smith, Mai Shore

as attendant to FN in the Crimea, 116–117, 120

as attendant to FN in London, 128, 132–133

inheritance of Mad Peter's estate, 17, 153

personality, 68

return to family, 140–141

support for FN's ambitions, 14, 29–30, 41, 71

travels with FN, 67–68

Smith, Octavius and Jane, 13–14

Smith, Patty, 14, 59

Index

Smith, Sam, 14, 30, 153

Smith, Shore

    birth, 14

    death and sale of Embley, 158

    FN's tutoring of, 40

    support for FN as Nightingale heir, 154

    support for FN's nursing ambitions, 64

Snow, John, 82

Somerville, Mary, 30, **31**

Sotheby, William, 30

Soyer, Chef Alexis

    description of FN, 105–106

    and military hospital food, 100–102, 113–114

    portrait, **101**

    soup kitchens, 100

    spa cures, 27, 61, 128, 141

Stanley, Mary, 45, 110–111

statistics, medical, 117, 129–131, **131**, 138

St. George, Sister, 90

St. Luke's Hospital for Lunatics, 78, **78**

St. Thomas's Hospital, 136–137, 151–152

Suggestions for Thought (Nightingale), 140, 143

Sutherland, Dr. John

    description of FN, 4

    friendship, collaborations with FN, 102, 129–130

    photograph, **103**

    work with sanitary commission, 102–103

telegraph, 84–85

Terrot, Sister Sarah Anne, 94

Thomas (drummer boy), 113, 122, **122**

Trautwein, Miss (Trout), 50

Turkish lantern, **107**

ventilation, fresh air, as cure for disease, 69, 81, 132, 139, 141, 147, 152

Verney, Sir Harry

    as advisor to/collaborator with FN, 134, 155

courtship of Parthe and marriage, 133–134

support for probationers, 152, **156**

support given by FN after Parthe's death, 157

Victoria, Queen of England

    ascension to the throne, 26, **27**

    death, 158

    descriptions of FN, 125, 155

    golden jubilee, 157

    honors given FN's parents, 107

    long reign, changes during, 26

    photograph, **126**

    reliance on Prince Albert, 125, 142

    scarves sent to Barrack Hospital, 100

    stamina-building exercises, 12

    visit with FN in Scotland, 123–126

Wardroper, Sarah Elizabeth (head nurse, Nightingale School), 137, 154–155, **156**

water cure, 67, 128, **128**, 141

women

    at Barrack Hospital, 92

    charity work, 18, 46, 55

    educational opportunities, 16, 29

    expectations for, 4, 134

    female doctors, 60

    importance of marrying well, 17, 30, 47

    importance of musical skills, 28

    independent, 4–6, 24, 60

    men's dominance over, 34, 46

    and need for active, meaningful work, 55–56, 140

    science studies, 30

    and social class, 10

workhouses, 145–149, **148**

wound care. *See also* Barrack Hospital, Scutari

    Lister's improvements in, 150–151

    as nursing function, 54, 85, 97, 136

Wyvill, Marmaduke, 33